DATE DUE

DEC 10'80			
OCT 1 5 1984			
APR 0 8 1988			
10-27-90 FEB 20 91			
NOV 7 2000			

DEMCO 38-297

PLANNING PROFITS IN THE FOOD AND LODGING INDUSTRY

PETER DUKAS

Jule Wilkinson, Editor

CAHNERS BOOKS
A Division of Cahners Publishing Company, Inc.
89 Franklin St., Boston, Massachusetts 02110
Publishers of Institutions/VF Magazine

ISBN 0-8436-2080-3

Printed in the United States of America

To

Aphrodite

and

Stephen

CONTENTS

LIST OF ILLUSTRATIONS

Preface

THE HOSPITALITY INDUSTRY is rich in its variety and complex in its segmentation. Given its role of service to the nation, that is the way it should be. Fortunately for the management of foodservice operations, there is a common body of administrative and operating concepts that form a unified structural framework.

As the sprawling, still-young giant of an industry continues its 2.5 billion dollar growth annually, the need for professional understanding and use of quantitative and qualitative data is vital. No foodservice operation, large or small, can rely on trial and error methods to survive, much less to prosper.

The concepts, procedures, and systems in this text, together with the analysis and presentation of quantitative data, should prove informative, and useful in a very practical way, to the newcomer in the field as well as to the experienced operator. The text is intended to have particular application to foodservice operations having less than $400,000 annual sales volume.

The comprehensive material on profit planning is divided into four major sections which should provide the serious reader with innovative, analytical tools and clear, step-by-step approaches that can increase profits significantly.

The first section introduces the necessary basic knowledge to evaluate and to use effectively the variety of information and tools provided by a general profit planning and expense control system.

The second section reviews present food cost control concepts, presents the modern approach to direct gross profit control, and summarizes the information necessary to plan food-sale profit centers.

In the third section, there is an analysis of present approaches to reduce payroll expense, and a presentation of new step-by-step methods to build increased profit through labor cost control.

The fourth section describes in detail a general system of liquor cost control that can and should be used by any operation *regardless* of size. It examines two major paths that an operator desiring more quantitative data may take for the cost control of alcoholic beverage consumption-and-sales, and for more profitable bar management.

Before proceeding in detail, I want to express my appreciation to Mr. William Cook and to Dianne Littwin of Hayden Publishing Co. for permission to abstract several specific pages and many of the concepts from my texts *How to Plan and Operate a Restaurant* and *Guide for Profitable Bar Management.* Turning to the editorial and publishing end of the work, I want to individually thank Mr. Myron Tucker, Brother Herman Zaccarelli, and Mr. William M. Woods of Cahners Books for their enthusiasm and interest in my writings, and for their suggestions and comments which resulted in a considerable improvement of this book. Finally, I would like to *try* to thank my wife for her great understanding and continuing patience and for the many ways she has helped me now and in the past.

For the last hour or so I have been searching my mind to remember one or more persons to whom I could shift responsibility for any errors contained in this book. Unfortunately, there were none.

PETER DUKAS

Section I
General Profit and
Expense Control Systems

Part 1 — A Personal Note

GOAL ACHIEVEMENT

THE STARSHIP THAT circles Mars and the leader who achieves his planned goals have two characteristics in common. They both have an inner guidance system that uses data to set a goal and to correct any deflection from their target—and they both move! The successful businessman determines long and short term goals, then acts. Guiding a business directly to its profit target requires a fund of knowledge as well as constant input of current data and, equally as important, reflection and thought.

THE VALUE OF INFORMATION

The significance of this text is not only in its presentation of information. Real value will come from critically analyzing the ideas, and then developing the ideas and data further. Moreover, information by itself has much less utility than is commonly supposed. To be effective, financial data should be viewed as a barometer, not as a record of the past; as a trend that may, and often will, continue in the future, not as a result, and as another tool pointing the way to solution of current problems.

Furthermore, only when the information is complete, valid, interpreted correctly, properly used, and the tentative solutions *made effective through action*, can information systems give a manager the direction and control he desires over his business.

THE POWER OF ACTION

The underlying, basic difference between success and failure is action. Unswerving direction toward goal and self-realization is paramount. There is no acceptable rationalization that excuses inaction—neither differences of intellectual ability nor health and emotional problems. Two businessmen with an I.Q. of 98 and 140 respectively, may be compared to two power boats, one with a 98 and the other with a 140 horsepower motor. Which boat will reach a target across the lake first? The answer depends on full utilization of potential. The smaller-powered boat will most certainly reach the specific point more quickly if the 140 h.p. boat gets a faulty start or has no rudder to direct its movement toward the target.

Unless we know the difference between wishful thinking and goal setting, and *use* that knowledge, we are not fit to care for a business. It is not enough to have truth planted in our minds; we must use the truth to rid our business of follies and mistakes.

The man who does not start will never move toward anything. It is infinitely better to try to do something and fail, than to do nothing and succeed.

A WORD OF CAUTION AND A WORD OF ENCOURAGEMENT

Every business will face its own rendezvous with destiny. The path taken at the crossroads will determine whether the end is rewarding and self-fulfilling or a punishing failure. The businessman who ignores changing consumer values and expectations, who stunts his mental growth and ceases to learn, who is unwilling to develop and professionally utilize his administrative and operative skills, will hardly survive his rendezvous with destiny.

On the other hand, the man who preserves his childhood enthusiasm and curiosity, who meditates on the many truths he has learned, who plans and uses his knowledge to better himself and his family, as well as his business and his community, who has intelligence cut in his features, character stamped on his brow, and love gleaming in his eyes—that man will meet destiny on his own terms.

Part 2 — Universal Approaches for Increased Profits

THERE ARE SEVERAL management methods that can be used to skillfully control profit. However, because most of these methods involve an understanding of expenses, the first step in profit control is to obtain necessary, detailed information of the various categories of expenses and of the means by which all expenses may be measured in a going operation.

CATEGORIES AND SIZE OF EXPENSE

Of the many classifications of expense, some are important and some relatively unimportant to profit control. The first six categories of expense that are of interest at this time are: size, control, occurrence, allocation, function, and stability.

Regarding size, the subcategories are major and minor expenses. If all other factors are equal, the more productive approach is to concentrate on major expenses first.

CONTROLLABLE AND NONCONTROLLABLE EXPENSE

The category of control includes controllable expense and noncontrollable expense. Obviously, analysis should be focused on controllable expense. Too often, in many operations, managers and owners waste time and energy on noncontrollable expenses such as interest, depreciation, taxes, rent, or other contractual obligations. The time to consider and do something positive about these expenses is *before* the decision is made to borrow money, or plan to maintain or accelerate depreciation *before* the lease or contract is signed.

VALUE OF OCCURRENCE

The expense category of occurrence can be subdivided into expenses that occur daily, frequently, periodically, or rarely.

This extremely important category is often overlooked. Consider: if an expense of only $10 that occurs daily can be eliminated or if a $10 reduction of a larger daily expense can be made, the immediate result is an increase of $3,650 on an annual basis! Moreover, if profits are 3 percent of sales, the $3,650 profit represents over $121,000 in sales. There are over 164,000 operations in the United States that cannot attain an annual sales volume of $120,000. The $10 expense elimination or reduction need be done only *one* time—during any one day or part of a day—to create the annual profit.

FACTORS IN ALLOCATION OF EXPENSES

The next category of expense is allocation. The subcategories to be emphasized here are *direct* and *indirect*. A restaurant has many different products for sale and may have several revenue and nonrevenue producing departments. However, if expenses are not analyzed to determine which are directly attributable to the product or to the department and which are not, no accurate measure of product or departmental efficiency can be made.

Allocation of expense is very seldom done uniformly, because it is slightly more complicated than is commonly supposed. Although it is easier to determine departmental direct expenses, some other expenses do present a problem. In an operation having a foodservice department, a bar, and a take-out department, rent or interest may be considered indirect expense. In this operation, if a waitress serves only food, her labor expense is a direct expense of the restaurant. However, if she also serves liquor, her expense can no longer be considered direct and should be separately classified as *joint* expense of the restaurant and bar. If music is piped into the dining room, the expense is direct for the restaurant. If it is played in both the dining room and the cocktail lounge, it is no longer direct. Another example: the expense of a menu that also has a wine list is a joint expense of the bar and the restaurant.

SOME VALUES IN ALLOCATING EXPENSES

If serious errors are made in the allocation of expenses to departments, consider how many more are made in product analysis. Why should the cost of specialized equipment, such as refrigerators, broilers, fryers, be allocated over all the food products in the restaurant? The refrigerator expense should be allocated directly to those items requiring refrigeration, the broiler expense to those items demanding broiling, and the frying expense to those items requiring frying. If these expenses are not allocated properly, there is no way to determine the cost of storing or preparing the product.

A final example is preparation labor. A prefabricated steak, a container of milk, a frozen or other convenience food purchased from an outside source require little or no preparation to serve. Yet many operators distribute their labor expense over all of the food items they sell. Is it any wonder that few know which items they make a profit on, or which items are being sold at a loss?

THE VALUE OF FUNCTION

The fifth category of expense is function, which serves to spotlight the responsibility for the expense on the particular department or activity that created or incurred the expense. Seemingly simple to do.

THE CATEGORY AND SUBCATEGORIES OF STABILITY

The last category in this introductory list of expenses is stability. Because this category answers the question as to what happens to expenses as sales volume fluctuates, it explains how profit can rise or fall because sales increase or decrease. When sales move in any direction and the dollar amount of expense remains the same, the expense is said to be fixed. On the other end of the scale, when sales move and the expense moves in the same direction and in the same proportion, the expense is said to be variable.

A semifixed expense stays fixed until sales reach a certain point, then it moves vertically in the same direction as sales. After the move, the semifixed expense again becomes fixed until continual pressure of sales movement forces it to move again. The best example of a semifixed expense is labor.

A semivariable expense moves in the same direction, but not in the same proportion, as sales. Food, kitchen fuel, utilities, telephone are good examples of semivariable expenses. As sales volume moves up or down, these expenses will increase or decrease, but not as much as sales.

Part 3—Six Different Methods
To Control Profits

SINCE PROFIT MAY be defined as the dollar value remaining after the deduction of all expenses from sales volume, the foodservice manager should realize that profit is a residual figure and cannot be controlled directly. The profit figure in any operation is manipulated by an understanding of the nature of that operation and by using the various factors that cause profits to fluctuate.

PROFITS AND EXPENSE REDUCTION

The simple formula, sales-minus-expenses-equals-profit, provides an understanding of some of the profit factors.

UNIT A

First Day		Second Day	
Sales	$100	Sales	$100
Expenses	90	Expenses	80
Profit	$ 10	Profit	$ 20

Unit A clearly demonstrates that one effective method of manipulating profit is to reduce expenses. Note also that the $10 reduction in expense created an immediate $10 increase in profit. This method is not only the fastest way to increase profits, but also needs to be done only one time to obtain the cumulative profit if the expense was previously incurred on a daily basis. (See the category of occurrence on p. 5.)

The following are the four basic steps to reduce expenses:

1. Select the expense you plan to reduce (concentrate first on major, controllable expenses that occur daily or frequently).

2. Before attempting to reduce the expense, determine whether it is necessary.

    a. Ask yourself why this expense was incurred.

    b. Is there a *better* way to accomplish the purpose?

    c. Break down the expense in detail and question each detail.

       (1) Can parts of the expense be combined or distributed to other necessary expenses?

       (2) Can parts be eliminated?

       (3) Why are these methods or materials used?

       (4) Where is the expense created? Why *there?*

       (5) Is it cheaper to purchase the value or to produce it?

       (6) Can the expenses be simplified so that the task can be done by an employee working at a lower rate of pay?

       (7) Can the expense be realized earlier or later?

       (8) Can the value be produced more cheaply by different equipment, by equipment instead of labor, or through a better layout?

3. If the cost is necessary, develop a new method.

    a. Investigate the entire expense as a whole. See if the entire department or unit can be eliminated or changed.

    b. Do away with unnecessary detail.

    c. Combine various elements of work.

    d. Re-arrange work for natural sequence.

    e. Pre-position tools, equipment, materials.

    f. Standardize product, ingredients, methods, tools, etc.

    g. Set up a standard budget.

    h. Work out and discuss ideas with all those who will be involved.

4. Apply new method; follow through.

    a. Set up time schedule for attaining objectives.

    b. Maintain a record of progress against this schedule periodically, so that you know the cost control program is operating effectively.

EXPENSE MANIPULATION AND PROFIT

There is no need to provide an example of profit control through expense manipulation. The reduction of expense mentioned earlier involves profit control through management decisions. For example, the decision to accelerate depreciation or to provide employees with medical and other benefits will result in a reduction of taxable income through management decision.

IMPORTANCE OF INCREASING SALES
VOLUME TO INCREASE PROFITS

To understand the role sales play in profits, study the following two examples.

UNIT A

First Day		Second Day	
Sales	$100	Sales	$200
Fixed expense	90	Fixed expense	90
Profit	$ 10	Profit	$110

UNIT B

First Day		Second Day	
Sales	$100	Sales	$200
Variable expense	90	Variable expense	180
Profit	$ 10	Profit	$ 20

In both examples, two unrealistic assumptions are made: all of the expenses of Unit A are fixed, and all of the expenses of Unit B are variable. These are the two extreme possibilities in the category of stability.

THE ROLE OF FIXED EXPENSES

In Unit A, since all expenses are fixed, the expenses will remain the same regardless of fluctuations in sales. Any increase in sales will result in an increase in profits. In this instance a doubling of sales resulted in a 110 percent increase of profits.

There is, of course, no operation that regards all in its expenses as fixed. However, the example clearly demonstrates that in any operation that has a high proportion of fixed-to-total expenses, the best method to increase profits is to increase sales. The example also explains why large hotels and motels have sales and convention departments, and restaurants with a lower proportion of fixed expenses do not.

THE ROLE OF FIXED AND OTHER EXPENSES

An interesting observation can be made by examining Unit B's profit and loss statement. In any foodservice operation there are many expenses that are fixed or scheduled such as interest, insurance, depreciation, taxes, or contractual obligations. In addition, the two major controllable expenses of labor and food are semifixed and semivariable respectively. Consequently, in all foodservice operations there are many expenses that stay the same as sales volume increases, and there are other expenses that move in the same direction, but *not* in the same proportion.

However, even when the unrealistic assumption is made that all expenses of an operation will not only increase, but also increase in the same proportion as sales, Unit B shows that a doubling of sales will double profits!

The profit and loss statements in Unit A and Unit B clearly demonstrate that any operation can increase its profits considerably by simply increasing its sales. To demonstrate this more effectively, study Unit C's profit and loss statement, one in which more realistic assumptions are made.

UNIT C

First Day			Second Day		
Sales		$100	Sales		$200
Food Cost 40%	$40		Food Cost 40%	$76	
Labor Cost	22		Labor Cost	30	
Kitchen fuel, utilities, etc.	8		Kitchen fuel, utilities, etc.	12	
Fixed Expense	20		Fixed Expense	20	
Total Expense		90	Total Expense		$138
Profit		$ 10	Profit		$ 62

Unit C has been averaging a 40 percent food cost at $100 sales volume. Since food cost is a semivariable expense, it will move in the same direction but not in the same proportion as sales. Food expense does not increase in the same proportion as sales for many reasons, including a better low cost sales mix, proportionally better utilization of food, lower cost per unit because of higher purchasing volume, smaller percentage of overproduction, less proportional waste in receiving, storing, issuing, production, and proportionally less loss through theft of food or sales as revenues increase.

Consequently, food expense cannot rise to $80 for that would mean that this expense is variable, and by definition it is semivariable. Since it is semivariable, it should increase as sales increase but to demonstrate the increased savings and proportionally smaller losses, food has been allowed to increase to $76.

Labor, a semifixed expense will increase at some point as sales volume increases, but certainly not as much as the semivariable expense of food. In this instance, a realistic increase is approximately $8 or 36 percent. Also, since the expenses of kitchen fuel and utilities are semivariable in nature, a 50 percent increase is sufficient.

Note the important part fixed expenses play in the profit picture. Fixed expenses on the first day are 20 percent of sales; but on the second day, because the sales volume doubled and fixed expenses remained the same, these expenses are only 10 percent of sales. In other words, $20 of the increased profit was created solely because fixed expense stayed the same as sales increased. The $35 additional profit was created because the semifixed and the semivariable expenses did not increase proportionally.

These examples establish that increasing sales volume in an operation materially increases profits. However, as a tool this method is too general.

THREE WAYS TO INCREASE SALES

Since sales is a function of number of customers times price (or the average check), profits can be increased by increasing the number of customers, varying prices, or increasing the average check. These factors then become three separate management tools to boost sales and, subsequently, profits.

Increasing the number of customers is a matter of investing time, energy, and/or money. People become customers because of quality food, reasonable prices, faultless service, attractive atmosphere, and good internal and external promotion of the operation.

The most effective way of handling prices is to relate continuously the prices of the menu items to what customers are willing to pay. A detailed discussion of pricing will be made later in this section.

For many foodservice operators, the average check per person is the net result of dividing sales volume by the number of customers. This is a very passive concept and affords little or no opportunity to increase sales. By studying the potential customer in terms of age, sex, occupation, income level, and propensity to consume; then by re-determining breakfast, lunch, and dinner check averages that will maximize profits for the restaurant and value for the customers, sales can be significantly increased.

Note, that since an average check per person can be increased without changing any menu prices, the average check is a separate tool that can be used to increase profits. There are several ways to increase the average check, e.g., the addition of an appetizer or dessert to the entree, the change of menu from a la carte to table d'hote, or the substitution on the table d'hote menu of one or more lower priced items for higher priced items.

Is there any way that profits may increase without increasing number of customers, prices, average check and without reducing or manipulating expense?

PROFITS AND THE SALES MIX

Some managers may not know that profits can be created through an effective menu or lost because of an improperly balanced menu. In any operation, as the customers shift from high cost items to low cost items, profits increase. If they select proportionally more high cost items, profits decrease.

In the table on the following page, the three menu items represent food groups that have a high, medium, and low food cost. The six customers could represent sixty or six hundred. Note that although there is recorded a 7 percent increase in profits on the second day, not one of the profit control tools was used. On both days there are six customers, the same menu prices, and the same average check. Also there was no change or reduction of expense by management.

The 40 cents additional profit on the second day does not seem significant until the observation is made that this increase was created by only 6 customers. If a more realistic customer count is used such as 600, the profit increase on the second day amounts to $40. In a thirty day period, provided the same proportionate menu selections are made, the additional profit would amount to $1,200.

If customers can change a profit picture by 7 percent, simply by selecting or not selecting low cost items on the menu, then management should not only make sure that each menu has a good balance of proportionally low cost items, but should also create an external and internal selling program that promotes the sale of these menu items.

TABLE 1—CHANGES IN SALES MIX

| | Item | | | 1st Day | | | 2nd Day | | |
	Cost	Price	%	No. Sold	Total Cost	Total Revenue	No. Sold	Total Cost	Total Revenue
Steak	.50	1.00	50	3	1.50	3.00	1	.50	1.00
Chicken	.40	1.00	40	2	.80	2.00	2	.80	2.00
Seafood	.30	1.00	30	1	.30	1.00	3	.90	3.00
Grand Total					2.60	6.00		2.20	6.00
Percentage					43.3		2nd day	36.6	
Gross Profit %					56.7			63.4	
					Difference	6.7			
Gross Profit $					3.40			3.80	
					Difference	.40			

Part 4—The Break-Even and Closing Points, Profit and Expense Control

BASIC PROBLEM OF PRE-PLANNED PROFIT AND EXPENSE CONTROL

REGARDLESS OF THE size of the expense or the size of the restaurant, most owners agree that the most profitable time to control expenses is *before* they are incurred, not after. The major problem appears to be the design and installation of an information system that is practical not only in terms of time, effort, and money, but also provides the owner with the information necessary to plan and predict expenses at varying sales volumes.

THE BREAK-EVEN POINT

USES OF BREAK-EVEN POINT

To plan expenses and profits properly each owner must know:

1. The amount of sales volume required to cover all the expenses

2. The amount of sales volume needed to obtain a given amount of profit

Because the break-even point answers these two important questions, it can be used for many other purposes, including the effect of increasing expenses on profits, for budgeting, forecasting, pre-planning of profits and expense, for making certain administrative and operating decisions, and for feasibility studies.

DEFINITIONS AND EXAMPLES

The break-even point is defined as the single point along the sales line where the total expense of an operation equals the total sales. Since total expenses and total sales are the same, there is no profit or loss in the operation and the operation breaks even. Hence, to determine the break-even point, all the manager must do is to discover the sales volume that equals total expenses.

Assume that "A" plans to open a restaurant. In addition to his salary, he desires $2,000 monthly profit. From past experience he anticipates the following monthly expenses:

Food Cost		40%
Labor Cost		25%
Light and Power	$400	
Kitchen fuel	100	
Cleaning and paper supplies	150	
Repairs and maintenance	100	
Miscellaneous		5%
Rent	2,000	
Depreciation	350	
Administrative and General	1,300	
Insurance	100	
Total expense	$4,500 +	70%

To ascertain whether or not he should go ahead with his plan, "A" must first determine the sales volume necessary to cover all of his expenses: the break-even point.

1. Total expenses equal 100 percent of sales at the break-even point.

2. $4,500 plus 70% = 100%

3. $4,500 = 100% − 70%

4. $4,500 = 30%

5. If $4,500 equals 30 percent of a figure, 100 percent equals $4,500 divided by 30 percent. Thus:

$$\frac{\$4,500}{.30} = \$15,000 \text{ total monthly expenses and monthly sales volume}$$

6. Inasmuch as $15,000 total expenses equal $15,000 total sales, the break-even point by definition equals $15,000.

To determine the sales volume needed to achieve his $2,000 monthly profit, "A" must add the desired profit to his total expenses.

1. Total expenses plus desired profit equal 100 percent of sales.

2. $4,500 + 70% + $2,000 = 100%

3. $4,500 + $2,000 = 100% − 70%

4. $6,500 = 30%

5. $$\frac{\$6,500}{.30} = \$21,666.66$$

According to his anticipated expenses, he now knows that he must locate his operation on a site that will provide him with a sales volume of over $21,660 monthly to make the desired profit, and a minimal sales volume of $15,000 to break even.

OTHER USES OF THE BREAK-EVEN POINT

The break-even point can be, and is, used by all industries for a variety of purposes, including forecasting and budgeting sales, expenses, cash flow requirements, profit planning; determining the effect of wage and other expense fluctuations, or of additions of new expense or capital items such as expansion, remodeling, alterations, or advertising programs.

USE BY THE HOTEL-MOTEL INDUSTRY

Of particular interest is the amount of specific management operational knowledge that can be obtained by the hotel and motel industry from this type of mathematical analysis. For example, assume that an experienced motel operator plans to build a 100-room motel in an area where motels have an annual occupancy of 70 percent and an average room rate of $14.00.

Because his motel is new, the motel owner believes he can achieve a 75 percent occupancy, operating 365 days a year with an average room rate of $14.00. He has determined that his capital or scheduled expense is $110,000 and his operating expenses are $46,700 plus 40 percent of sales. He desires to net $1,000 per room or $100,000 annually. With this information, can he determine if his plan is feasible or could be made feasible with a few changes?

The break-even point is 100 percent of all the expenses, (40% + $46,700 + $110,000).

$$100\% = 40\% + 156,700$$
$$100\% - 40\% = \$156,700$$
$$60\% = \$156,700$$

If 60 percent of a figure is $156,700, 100 percent of that amount is $156,700, divided by .60 or $261,166. Therefore, the break-even point is $261,166 (approximately 51 percent occupancy).

The motel owner now knows that he will break even if he sells 51 rooms or has an occupancy of 51 percent. Since all the motels in the area have an average of 70 percent occupancy and his motel will be newer and more competitive, he is no longer concerned with either the break-even or the closing point.

He must now determine his net profit at his projected 75 percent occupancy and calculate the sales volume and occupancy necessary to generate his desired net profit of $100,000 annually.

1. The maximum sales volume possible, 100 percent occupancy, is the number of rooms times the average room rate times the number of operating days. Therefore, the maximum sales volume is 100 x $14 x 365, or $511,000.

2. At 75% occupancy the sales volume is $383,250. At this sales volume the total expenses are 40% of $383,250 + $156,700, or total expenses = $153,300 + $156,700 = $310,000. Therefore, his profit is $383,250 - $310,000, or $73,250.

3. Evidently he can net $73,250 with 75% occupancy. However, the motel operator had planned to net $100,000. If total expenses and average room rate remain substantially fixed, what sales volume is required to obtain the $100,000 net profit?

to the total expenses of	40% + $156,700
add the profit desired	$100,000
therefore, the required sales volume is	40% + $256,700

Since $256,700 is equal to 60 percent of the required sales volume, sales must reach $427,833!

A $427,833 volume is over 83 percent occupancy. Therefore, if expenses and average room rate remain as they are now, the $100,000 net is unattainable. Evidently, either the capital expenditures must be reduced or the average room rate increased. Because the change in the average room rate can produce additional information of interest, the decision is made to increase room rates.

Since the sales volume necessary to net $100,000 is $427,833 and the number of rooms available for sale at 75 percent occupancy is 27,375, all that is required to determine the new average room rate is to divide the number of rooms, 27,375, into the required sales volume, $427,833. The new average room rate is $15.6286.

This rate is an average and does not provide the information necessary to set the room rate for single or double occupancy. Assume that the motel owner expects 80 percent of his rooms will be double occupancy and the difference between the single and the double room rate is $6.00. Accordingly, the single and double room rates can be determined by designating the single room as x, the double room as x+6, and equating these rates with the equivalent average room rate.

For example, since 80 percent of the rooms have more than one occupant, the number of rooms sold as singles must equal 20 percent. Therefore, in simple form:

$$8(x+6) + 2(x) = \$156.29$$
$$8x + \$48 + 2x = \$156.29$$
$$10x = \$156.29 - \$48.00$$
$$10x = \$108.29$$
$$x = \$ 10.83, \text{ the single rate}$$
$$x+6 = \$ 16.83, \text{ the double rate}$$

DETERMINATION AND USE OF DAILY BREAK-EVEN POINT

Earlier in this chapter, the importance and use of the monthly break-even point were described. Also covered were a variety of uses of budgeting and profit planning for determining the effect that expense or cost fluctuations, or additions, would have on profit. On another operational level, the substantive additional information provided by a *daily* break-even point and a closing point of the operation is equally important.

In combination, analysis of these two points of sales volume by the owner can decide the pricing structure and the average check, and the feasibility of an additional expense as a merchandising tool (renting equipment to put on a buffet for family dining on Sunday, for example), can provide a management tool for competition, and can determine whether or not it is profitable to stay open for business on any one day, or for any one particular meal period.

To determine the break-even point (or the sales volume needed to achieve the desired profit on a *daily basis*) all that is necessary is to divide the pertinent figures on the monthly profit and loss statement by the number of operating days; or if the monthly break-even point and profit figures have been obtained, divide these figures by the number of operating days in the month.

For example, using the figures of "A's" foodservice operation: the monthly break-even point and the desired monthly

profit sales volume are $15,000 and $21,666.66 respectively. Assume the number of operating days this month is thirty: the *daily* break-even point is:
$$\frac{15,000}{30} = \$500$$

and the daily sales volume required to make $2,000 monthly profit (or its equivalent, $66.67 daily profit) is:
$$\frac{21,666.66}{30} = \$722.22$$

DEFINITION AND EXPLANATION OF THE CLOSING POINT

The closing point of an operation can be defined as that point when sales volume fails to recover all the costs of opening the restaurant for business. For example, separate the expenses of a restaurant into two groups. In the first group, place expenses that continue whether the restaurant is closed for one month, one day, or even one meal period. In the second group, place the expenses that are incurred when a decision is made to open for business.

Typical examples of continuous expenses are rent, (when it is a fixed dollar amount), depreciation, interest, taxes, insurance premiums, contractual obligations, administrative and general costs, refrigeration, etc. Operational expenses—those costs that will be incurred because the decision is made to open for business—are food, labor, lights, power, kitchen fuel, cleaning and paper supplies, repairs and maintenance, and any expense based on a percentage of sales.

If it will cost the operator $100 to open the door for business, he must obtain at least $100 in sales. In the event that sales drop to $90, he will lose $10 that could have been saved if he had stayed closed!

Returning to the prior analysis of "A" and his foodservice operation, let us speculate that "A" opens his restaurant and for a few months sales are as anticipated. Then, gradually, sales volume begins a steady decline from $22,000 to $15,000, $12,000, $8,000, $4,000, finally $2,000. At what point in a rapidly declining sales market should he have closed his operation? Inasmuch as the break-even point is $15,000, he could have continued indefinitely at $15,000 sales volume. At that point, although there is no profit, the sales volume generated covers all the expenses of the operation, including his salary.

Use and Examples

In "A's" operation a study of his profit and loss statement indicates that every month he decides to be open for business his average expenses are:

Food		40%
Labor		25%
Lights and power	$400	
Kitchen fuel	100	
Cleaning and paper supplies	150	
Repairs and maintenance	100	
Miscellaneous expense		5%
Total cost of staying open	$750	+70%

1. $750 + 70\% = 100\%$ (the cost of opening)
2. $750 = 100\% - 70\%$
3. $750 = 30\%$
4. $\dfrac{\$750}{.30} = \$2,500 =$ monthly costs of being open.

Additionally, let us assume that the monthly expenses that continue regardless of whether the restaurant is open or not, total $3,750. At the break-even point, $15,000 sales volume, *all* expenses, continuous and operating, are covered so this comfortable sales volume will not be considered. Consider, however, that for three successive months sales volume is $4,000, $2,500, and $2,000 respectively.

Sales	$4,000	$2,500	$2,000
Expense	70% + $750	70% + $750	70% + $750
of being	$2,800	$1,750	$1,400
open	+750	+750	+750
Total	$3,550	$2,500	$2,150
Expense of			
being open			
Difference	+450	0	(150)

The sales of $4,000, $1,500 above the closing point ($2,500), created $450 additional revenue over operating expenses. Because he did not remain closed that month, his continuous expenses of $3,750 were reduced by $450 and are now only $3,300. Instead of losing $3,750, he lost only $3,300. It is advantageous to be open for business anywhere below the break-even point so long as sales volume does not drop below the closing point.

To demonstrate this, consider the amount of total loss when sales volume is the same $4,000.

Sales $4,000
Total expenses   70% plus $4,500   ($3,750 continu-
                     $2,800   ous expenses plus
                     +4,500 $750 lights, pow-
Total expenses $7,300   er, fuel, etc.)
        loss ($3,300)

USES OF THE BREAK-EVEN AND CLOSING POINTS COMBINATION

To repeat, when total expenses are considered, the continuous expenses of $3,750 are reduced to $3,300 proving that it is advantageous to be open for business any time that forecasted sales are above the closing point. However, unlike the break-even point at which a business can continue operating indefinitely, no business can continue indefinitely below the break-even point and above the closing point. In this instance the $3,300 loss is a real loss and provides a warning.

The sales volume of $2,500 the second month is the closing point and will not be evaluated. Sales of $2,500 equal the cost of staying open ($2,500 operational expenses); thus, the loss of $3,750 of continuous expenses is not affected.

In the third month, sales dropped below the closing point to $2,000 dollars. In addition to the $3,750 continuous expenses, the operator has incurred a loss of $150 by staying open. His total expenses are now $3,900. By staying closed that month "A" could have saved himself a great deal of time, effort, anxiety, and $150!

GRAPHIC PRESENTATIONS OF BREAK-EVEN AND CLOSING POINTS

A graph portraying not only the break-even and closing points, but also the interplay of total expenses from zero to maximum sales volume, is a very important tool at management disposal. All expense or sales relationships are revealed by visual inspection instead of detailed mathematical analysis.

TWO METHODS USED TO CONSTRUCT GRAPHS

Two methods of constructing this type of graph are explained in the pages that follow. The first method is based on analysis and subsequent grouping of expense. Because it is slightly more accurate than the second method, it should be utilized by the exacting manager. The second method requires only 3 or 4 consecutive profit and loss statements, from which the manager isolates sales, profit, and scheduled or fixed expenses, to construct a graph accurate within $5 to $8. Both graphs can be used effectively for the same purposes.

DIRECTIONS, EXAMPLES, PROOFS,
AND USES OF THE FIRST METHOD

To avoid considerable repetition, the detailed directions for graph construction are discussed in the construction of the graph using the second method, and the mathematical analysis and proofs of the pictorial representations on the graphs are detailed only for the first graph. The manager of restaurant A selects a current profit and loss statement that contains no unusual expense and is fairly typical of the operation; studies each expense item to determine if the expense is one that is incurred because the operation is open for business on any one day; separates those expenses from the fixed or scheduled expenses that will continue to be incurred even if the operation is closed, and concludes that the following data is typical for his foodservice unit.

Operation or Opening expense $54.00 plus 70%
Scheduled expense   66.00
   Total expenses $120.00 plus 70%

Since his maximum daily sales the past six months have been $520, he decides to construct a graph depicting $600 sales and $600 expense. On graph paper he draws a large square (see completed graph shown on page 24), identifies the bottom of the square as a sales scale, the left side as an expense scale, and draws a sales line diagonally beginning at zero sales to the upper right-hand corner of the graph. The sales volume at any point along the sales line is read by referring to the sales scale. The total expenses at any sales volume are read by referring to the expense scale on the left side of the graph. (Each small square on the graph represents $20.)

The manager first plots the "opening" expense, in this case, $54.00 plus 70%, and then the scheduled expense of $66.00 on the expense scale. Because at zero sales seventy percent of zero is zero, the opening expense at zero sales must be $54. Therefore, beginning at zero sales and moving up the expense scale, a dot is placed 2-7/10 squares up, to represent the

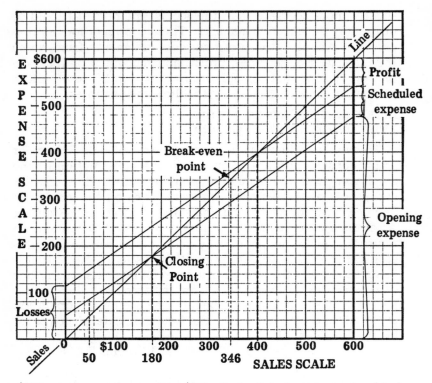

$54 opening expense. The $66 of scheduled expenses is added to the $54 by placing a dot on the expense scale that represents $120 expenses. (54+66)

The only remaining mathematics involved is the determination of the break-even point (B.P.). Therefore, since

B.P. is equal to 100% sales volume (X) when X equals total expenses

B.P. = 100% = $120 + 70%

B.P. = 100% – 70% = $120

B.P. = 30% = $120

B.P. = $400 (.30/$\overline{120.00}$ = 400)

A dot is placed on the sales line at that point that represents $400. A straight line is drawn from the total expense dot representing $120 to the $400 sales dot and extended to the right side of the graph. This establishes the total expense line for the restaurant from zero to $600 sales.

From the dot on the expense scale representing the $66 of scheduled expense, a parallel line is drawn below the total expense line extending from the expense scale to the right side of the graph. The graph is now complete. The distance below the total expense line to the scheduled expense line is the same along the entire length of the lines, since the lines are parallel to each other, and represents $66 of scheduled expense. The area *below* the scheduled expense line represents the opening or operational expense of the restaurant.

Merely by glancing at the chart, the manager of restaurant A now has a tool that will provide him with a great deal of important information. For example:

- Since the break-even point is that point in sales volume where total sales equal total expenses, the break-even point is at the intersection of the total expense line and the sales line—this is the only place where total sales equal total expenses—$400.
- The closing point of an operation is that point where total sales equal the cost of being open. The graph shows that only at the $180 sales volume does total sales equal the expense of opening. Therefore, $180 must be the closing point (C.P.) of the operation.

  Proof:

$$\text{C.P.} = 100\% \text{ sales} = 70\% + \$54$$
$$\text{C.P.} = 100\% - 70\% = \$54$$
$$\text{C.P.} = 30\% = \$54$$
$$\text{C.P.} = \$180 \ (30\overline{)5400} = \$180)$$

- In this operation $66 of expense will continue even if the operation is closed for any one day. Consequently, the graph depicts that if sales are above the closing point of an operation, sales revenue is greater than opening expense. As a result, scheduled expenses are reduced by an amount equal to the distance from a point on the sales line down to the opening expense line. Also, if sales fall below the closing point, in addition to the scheduled expense of $66, expenses will exceed revenue by an amount equal to the distance traversed by a straight vertical line from any point on the sales line below the closing point, to its respective opposite point on the scheduled expense line.

The examples on the graph indicate that if sales are projected at only $54, "A" will incur not only the scheduled expenses of $66 but also an additional $39 to $40 he could have saved by not opening for business that day. At projected sales of $340 (below the break-even point but above the closing point) the manager should open for business because if he closes he will lose $66 of scheduled expenses. Open, he will lose approximately $16.

Proof (below the closing point):

Sales volume	$50

Cost of opening 70% + $54 = 100%

$$\$54 = 100\% - 70\%$$
$$\$54 = 30\%$$

therefore 100% =	$89
Loss	$39
Plus loss of scheduled expense	$66
Total loss	$105

Proof (above the closing point):

Sales volume	$346
Less opening expense (70% + $54) =	$296
Difference	50
Less scheduled expense	66
Loss is now only	$ 16 (instead of $66 had the operation remained closed for business that day)

No additional mathematical proofs should be required. An experienced observer of the graph can rely on the variety of information provided without burdensome, extensive computations or mathematical proofs of accuracy. To illustrate, a visual inspection of the graph indicates that at a $500 sales figure the operation will average $30 profit.

When sales volume is:	$240	$450	$600
(Loss) or profit is:	(48)	$ 15	$ 60

When sales volume is $540 and $40 respectively, what is this operation's profit or (loss)? A look at the graph should indicate the answer.

The preceding graph is a pictorial representation of the closing point. A detailed study of the line relationships will provide management with much more detailed information than the few examples provided in these pages. The examples that were given of the variances in profit or loss or sales volume fluctuations, are mathematical proofs of the information the graph clearly depicts as the sales and cost lines intersect and diverge.

DISCUSSION AND DIRECTIONS FOR SECOND METHOD

Since this is so, often it is not necessary to spend a considerable amount of time, energy, and money analyzing each expense and placing it in its particular cost group. Any manager can use the simplified second method to construct a break-even and closing point graph that will provide the same desired information, accurate within $5 to $8. All that is required to make this graph is a scaled graph paper, three or four consecutive profit and loss statements, and a total of the expenses that an operation will continue to incur even if the operation is closed for any one day.

To illustrate, foodservice operation A has 4 consecutive profit and loss statements that provide the following information for the graph:

Total scheduled expenses are $90 daily.

Daily sales the past four months have averaged $400, $550, $470 and $675 respectively.

Daily profit or (loss) the past four months has averaged ($50), $20, ($10), and $75 respectively.

Steps in making the graph:

1. On a graph paper, the scale of the one illustrated on page 28 ($25 for each square), scale 9 to $800 on any bottom, horizontal line.

2. Beginning at the zero sales line, scale an $800 vertical expense line.

3. Complete the perfect square by extending a horizontal line from the $800 expense square and a vertical line from the $800 sales square until the lines intersect.

4. Draw a straight sales line from zero to the upper right-hand corner. (Any point along this sales line can be read by extending a visual line vertically down from the point until it intersects with the sales scale.)

5. Plot each of the stated profits or losses according to their respective sales volumes by placing a dot representing the amount in dollars from the sales line. For example, when sales volume was $675, profit was $70. From the $675 point on the sales line deduct 2-4/5 squares (each square represents $25) and place a dot.

Also when sales were $425, the operation incurred a loss of $50. Therefore, a dot is placed two squares above, the point representing $425 on the sales line.

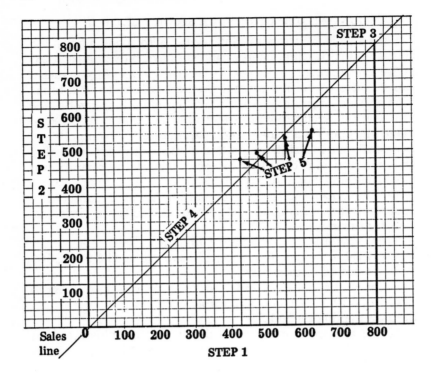

6. Draw a single straight line from the left to the right side of the graph so that the line passes as close as possible to all the dots that have been plotted. This creates a moving average and represents the total expenses of the operation. At any point where the total expense line falls below the sales line, the vertical distance between the two lines measures profit. At any point where the total expense line is above the sales line, the vertical distance between the two lines measures loss.

Notice that the sales and total expense lines intersect at only one point on the graph. At that point, on this graph approximately $515, there is no distance between the two lines. Therefore, there is no profit or loss. Consequently, $515 is the break-even point.

7. To portray the closing point on this graph, subtract from the total expense line the $90 scheduled expenses. (A point on the total expense line is valued and determined by drawing a visual line horizontally from the point to the expense scale.)

At zero sales, this restaurant will incur $90 of expense that

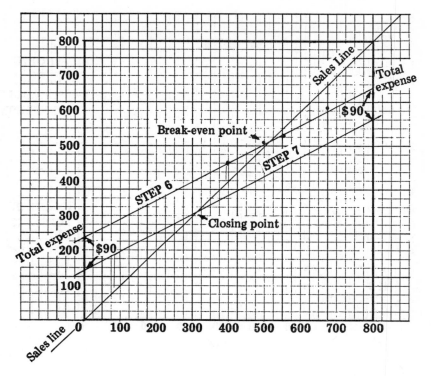

is scheduled to continue regardless of whether or not it is open for business. Therefore, subtract $90 from the total expense line at zero sales, place a dot, and draw a line parallel to the total expense line. Obviously, the vertical distance between the two lines at any point along the length of the two lines is exactly $90 and measures the amount of scheduled expenses that will go on even if the operation stays closed.

On the other hand, if this is so, the entire area below the scheduled expenses must be all of the remaining expenses that are incurred because the decision is made to open for business on any one day.

VARIETY OF INFORMATION PROVIDED BY GRAPHS

For all purposes, the graph has been completed. The further identification shown on graph on p. 30, is to provide increased understanding of the graph and its use as a management tool. For example, the intersections at numbers 2 and 6 point out that the closing and break-even points for this operation are

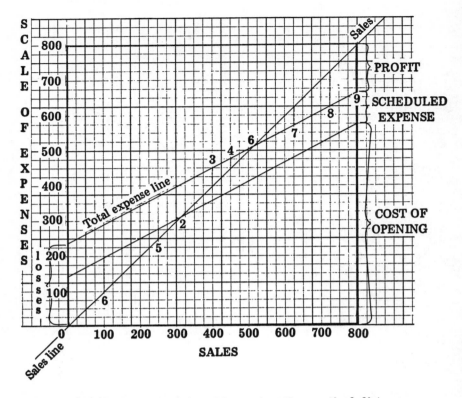

$320 and $515 respectively. Measuring the vertical distance between sales and the total expense line at numbers 7, 8, and 9, tells management that if sales reach $625, $750, or $800 a day, the owner will net $50, $100, and $135 profit respectively.

Since numbers 3 and 4 are between the closing and break-even point, the owner should remain open even if he anticipates a sales volume of only $450 or $400. If he closes the operation, he will lose only $30 at the $450 sales volume and $50 at the $400 sales volume. Note how readily the information is obtained by determining the vertical distance between the sales line and the total expense line.

At any sales volume below the closing point, the sales line moves below the scheduled expense area into the cost of being open area. This immediately informs the owner that not only will he lose the $90 expenses that are scheduled; but also, that the revenue he obtains from sales will be less than the expense of being open. The greater the vertical distance is between the sales line and the total expense line, the larger the loss. For example, at $100 and $250 sales volume, numbers 6 and 5, he will lose not only the $90 scheduled expense but also an additional $95 and $30 respectively.

Part 5—The Design and Use of the Profit and Loss Statement

THE IMPORTANCE OF THE PROFIT AND LOSS STATEMENT

THE PROFIT AND LOSS statement—if it is designed and used properly—is one of the most powerful instruments that the manager has to help him make the productive decisions necessary to create a dynamic, profitable, increasingly successful business. Adherence to four basic rules can transform this financial record from a document used only for reporting taxable income, to a report on sales and costs and their trends, a gauge of revenue-producing units and departmental productivity, an accurate measure of managerial efficiency and responsibility, a basis for preparing operating budgets and effective distribution of expense, a means to establish administrative control over all activities, a data bank to establish break-even and closing points—*and* a report of taxable income.

FOUR BASIC RULES TO INCREASE VALUE

The Four Basic Rules to increase value are:
1. Compare two or more profit and loss statements that measure equal time periods.
2. Separate all expenses into two categories; controlled and scheduled expenses.
3. Group and assign sales and all direct expenses to their respective departments.
4. Describe each major sales and expense item as dollars and as a percentage.

VALUE OF EQUAL PERIODS

Unless two consecutive profit and loss statements contain an equal number of days—peak volume days and low volume days—the statements will be very difficult to compare. How does an operator compare sales or expenses in one period that has 28 days with another period that has 31 days? How does the owner of a restaurant compare one statement that contains five Saturdays and five Sundays with another statement that contains only four?

In the profit and loss statement that follows, the comparative time columns (identified as "last month," "this month" in a typical statement) were deliberately designated as "January" and "February" to dramatize the value of equal periods, and to demonstrate the inaccurate and misleading conclusions that may be drawn. Food sales, for example, are listed as $32,000 in January and $30,000 in the month of February, an obvious drop in sales volume of $2,000.

This decrease in sales volume, which is so apparent, in reality hides a very real increase in food sales of $1,105. Since February has only 28 days and January 31 days, the average daily sales for February are $1,072 and in January only $1,032, a $39.41 daily *increase* in food sales. Over the 28-day period in February, food sales have increased $1,105 dollars! The reason management can very easily arrive at misleading conclusions and poor decisions is that they will forget they are not comparing two equal periods.

A much more useful profit and loss statement could be based on a 13-month year, or a four-week period. Also, if the statement began on the same day that the weekly payroll began, problems of accruals or deferrals would be largely eliminated.

The 28-day period for the profit and loss statement has one serious disadvantage: the information comes 28 days late. If management eliminated all fixed, scheduled, and periodic expenses, and concentrated on the expenses that are incurred in any one day, a simplified but very valuable daily gross profit and loss statement could be evolved.

In any event, the value of comparing equal time periods needs no further elaboration. So, to facilitate meaningful analysis of the data contained in the financial statement shown on pages 34-35, the columns designated January and February should now be regarded as two equal periods of time, each period containing 28 days.

USE OF DOLLAR AND PERCENTAGE FIGURES

The requirement that each major sales and major expense item should be described in dollar amounts and in percentages

TABLE 2—COMPARATIVE OPERATING STATEMENT FOR CURRENT PERIOD, PAST PERIOD, AND YEAR TO DATE

	FEB.		JAN.		TO DATE	
	Amount	*%*	*Amount*	*%*	*Amount*	*%*
SALES: Food	30,000	74.0	32,000	76.1	62,000	75.0
Bar	10,000	24.6	9,000	21.4	19,000	23.0
Other	500	1.2	1,000	2.3	1,500	1.7
TOTAL SALES	40,500	100	42,000	100	82,500	100
COST OF SALES: Net Food Cost	12,000	40.0	13,440	42.0	25,440	41.0
Net Bar Cost	3,000	30.0	2,520	28.0	5,520	29.0
Other Cost	250	50.0	500	50.0	750	50.0
TOTAL COST OF SALES	15,250	37.4	16,460	39.1	31,710	38.2
GROSS PROFIT	25,250	62.6	25,540	60.8	50,790	61.7
CONTROLLED EXPENSES:						
Payroll - Food Department	6,000	20.0	6,760	18.0	12,760	19.0
Bar	1,000	10.0	810	9.0	1,810	9.5
Other	150	30.0	150	15.0	300	22.5
Administrative, Mgt.	2,025	5.0	2,016	4.8	4,041	4.9
Administrative, Clerical	810	2.0	881	2.1	1,691	2.05
Employee Meals	1,215	3.0	1,386	3.3	2,601	3.15
Payroll Tax	200		225		425	

Utilities	400		445		845	
Repairs & Maintenance	350		407		757	
Advertising	500		600		1,100	
Travel Expense	250		225		475	
Paper Supplies	200		185		385	
Menus & Stationery	100		150		250	
Clean & Other Supplies	100		100		200	
TOTAL CONTROLLED EXPENSES	13,300	32.8	14,340	34.1	27,640	33.5
PROFIT AFTER CONTROLLED EXPENSES	11,950	29.5	11,200	26.6	23,150	28.06
SCHEDULED EXPENSES:						
Rent	2,025	5.0	2,025	4.8	4,050	4.9
Insurance	500	1.23	500	1.1	1,000	1.2
Licenses	2,025	5.0	2,025	4.8	4,050	4.9
Interest & Bank Charges	1,015	2.5	1,015	2.4	2,030	2.45
Depreciation	2,025	5.0	2,025	4.8	4,050	4.9
TOTAL SCHEDULED EXPENSES	7,590	18.7	7,590	18.0	15,180	18.35
TOTAL ALL COSTS & EXPENSES	36,140	89.3	38,390	91.4	74,530	90.35
NET PROFIT BEFORE INCOME TAX	4,360	10.7	3,610	8.6	7,970	9.65

indicates that data expressed only in dollars or only in percentages is very misleading. It is quite possible for a dollar figure to increase and the same figure expressed as a percentage to decrease. The reverse is also very possible. Accordingly, some poor conclusions may be drawn and unwise decisions made, when data is not expressed in dollar amounts as well as percentages so that more than one relationship is revealed.

Moreover, a blanket percentage figure such as 30 percent labor cost for the entire operation is generally useless as a management tool. A blanket percentage figure tells what happened, but does not tell what created the cost, if it was necessary, or where the cost was incurred.

Notice that percentages alone do not tell the entire story. Percentage data must be compared to the dollar value. In the food department's payroll, for example, the labor cost percentage shows a rise of two percent. However, when this is compared with the dollar value of the payroll, the manager effected a savings of $760.

Several items on the statement do not have percentage values. The reason for this omission is to illustrate that any percentage figure used must be of value to management. If a manager cannot use the information, there is not much sense in incurring expense to accumulate data that is not, or cannot be, used to tighten the control of the operation.

For this reason, also, several percentage figures shown were not carried out to the last decimal point. Why should any figure containing percentages always total 100 percent? What good does it do management to know that a certain expense varied one hundredth of a percentage point?

The percentage figures shown in the scheduled expense columns are also meaningless from a comparative standpoint. Since all of the expenses are fixed dollar-wise, a percentage fluctuation of 100 percent is indicative of a *sales* volume increase or decrease, not a fluctuation in *cost*.

REASONS FOR SEPARATING CONTROLLABLE EXPENSES

This statement is deliberately designed to record and emphasize those costs that can and should be controlled by competent management. In addition to the item, Cost of Sales, all expenses listed under the heading Controlled Expenses can be controlled and should be the main responsibility of the manager. His effectiveness in operating a foodservice operation can be measured accurately and definitely in direct proportion to his ability to increase his sales and reduce the cost of sales or any excessively high controllable expense.

Below the controlled expense category are scheduled expenses. This classification includes all expenses that, because of some law or prior agreement with outside agencies such as local and state governments, banks, and landlords, are relatively fixed and pre-determinable. The time to consider these expenses is before they are incurred. After a law is passed or a ruling has been made regarding valuation of real property, licenses, taxes, or when an agreement is reached concerning the amount of rent, depreciation, insurance, or interest expense, the cost passes beyond the immediate control of the operating manager.

VALUE OF SEPARATING EXPENSES BY CLASSIFICATION

The immediate value of this classification is that any owner can glance at his statement and know instantly how productive he or his manager is. Without this classification of expense, the costs that are a manager's responsibility are distributed over the entire profit and loss statement. With the customary format, one item of cost is pointed out at a time and then another cost is located and discussed. This is not only time-consuming, but also indicates a lack of organization and faulty cost distribution.

A profit and loss statement should not only dramatically emphasize those costs that are the manager's responsibility but also provide him with an accurate index of his ability as the operating head of his unit. The classification of expenses as shown in the illustrated operating statement will achieve both those objectives.

The most significant features of the operating statement are not that they provide a record of sales and costs—more important than this is the fact that the sales and costs have been pinpointed, summarized in a single, easily comprehensible digest for evaluation, and spotlighted as the sole responsibility of the operating manager.

Once the competent operating manager realizes that these records provide the owners with a comprehensive index of his ability and make him solely responsible for abnormal fluctuations in sales, food, labor, and other controllable costs, he will use these statements as valuable, additional tools to increase his efficiency and to assure the success of the foodservice operation for which he is being held responsible.

THE ALLOCATION OF DIRECT EXPENSES

The rule regarding grouping and assigning sales and direct expenses to their respective departments involves the familiar category of allocation that was discussed previously in Part 2 of this section. Once again the problem is to study each expense and determine if the expense is unquestionably direct and can be allocated to one particular department.

The determination and allocation of direct expenses to their respective revenue- or nonrevenue-producing departments is very seldom done uniformly and is probably a little more complicated than is commonly supposed. However, if this allocation is not made, there will not be an accurate, reliable measure of the cost of operating any department or the determination of the actual gross profit of a revenue-producing department. There is no other more effective method to determine departmental productivity.

Notice that the departmental sales figures give management considerably more information than the gross sales figure alone can give. The gross sales figures point out that sales have dropped $1,500 in February compared to January's operation. Thus, gross sales data reveals only trends in total sales. The departmental sales figures, however, show a $2,000 loss in food sales, a $1,000 increase in bar sales, and a 50 percent decrease in "other sales." This specific information pinpoints a definite area. In contrast to the general information provided by gross sales figures, the departmental data tells the manager not only *what* happened but *where*.

Knowing the area of trouble, the manager can now direct his attention to the proper revenue-producing department and discover the cause for drop in sales. Did sales drop in the food department because of poor quality food, a change in menu prices, poor service, inadequate promotion? Now that we know *where* to look, we can find *what* the trouble is and eliminate it.

DEPARTMENTAL PRODUCTIVITY

To determine the relative productivity of each revenue-producing department is also very simple with this type of statement. The total columns point out that up to this time in the current accounting period, the food department has accounted for 75 percent of the gross sales; the bar, 23 percent of gross sales; and "other sales," less than 2 percent. The cost-of-sales section in the to-date columns reports that in order to obtain $100 worth of sales, the food department spent $41 for food, the bar only $29 for liquor, and the "other" revenue-producing departments $50. Stated simply, for every $100 sales, the food department contributed $59 to the gross profit, the bar $71, and the "other" revenue-producing department only $50.

The figures become even more practical and interesting when the direct labor cost of each department is added to the respective cost of sales. For every $100 in sales, after cost of sales and labor are deducted, the food department contributed only $40 to pay for other expenses, the bar $61, and the "other" revenue-producing department only $27.50. The bar is obviously the most productive and the "other" revenue-producing department the least.

The cost of sales figures in the February and January columns emphasize the importance of the bar to gross profit. Although bar cost for February was 2 percent higher than January, an 11 percent increase in sales resulted in an additional $520 bar contribution to gross profit—almost 21 percent higher than its previous base.

Each restaurateur has his own ideas on policy formulation. One may want to emphasize food sales and another to emphasize liquor sales. Whatever the case may be, the comparative operating statement points out that if promotional costs are the same for both the restaurant and the bar, the gross return on advertising expense necessary to create an additional $100 in sales is $40 from food sales and $61 from bar sales.

GROSS PROFIT ANALYSIS

Although a $1,500 decrease in sales was recorded in February, the gross profit percentage figure shows an increase of 1.8 percent. Generally, the reverse is true—as sales decrease, expenses increase. What happened in this operation that created an increase in potential profit? Was it due to the manager's ability? Was it caused by a shift in sales? If the cause for the increase is determinable, we may be able to duplicate the condition again.

Since gross profit is the deduction of cost of sales from sales, an analysis of changes in gross profit involves an analysis of changes in sales and in cost of sales. In this case, February food sales were $30,000, and food cost was 40 percent or $12,000. If the manager had not actively intervened, the food cost percentage for February would have been 42 percent, or $12,600. One reason for the percentage increase of gross profit, therefore, is the additional $600 saved from cost of the food.

February bar sales increased $1,000 over January, and bar cost rose to 30 percent during the same period. The bar sales and cost figures show, however, that the net bar contribution to gross profit in January was only $6,480 compared to the $7,000 contribution made in February. Consequently, gross profit was increased by $520.

DEPARTMENTAL PERFORMANCE STANDARDS

The calculations above bring us close to a subject dear to the hearts of many competent restaurant operators—the establishment and maintenance of proper departmental standards. For example, on the basis of the operating statement shown, what should the food cost percentage be? As an owner, should we ask the manager to maintain a 40 percent food cost, a 42 percent food cost, or take the average of 41 percent?

Closer study of the profit and loss statement shows that during January when food costs were 42 percent, sales were $32,000. In February, however, a 40 percent food cost grossed only $30,000 food sales. Is this information significant? Which is better for the operation, $32,000 sales volume at 42 percent or a $30,000 volume at 40 percent food cost? Dollar-wise, the 42 percent cost contributes $18,560 to gross profit and the 40 percent cost contributes only $18,000, a difference of $560 a month.

The problem of determining the proper standard, therefore, is to determine what caused the decrease in sales. Did food sales drop because there was a change in menu pricing, a shift from larger to smaller portions, or a change in quality? Almost anyone can reduce costs in this manner. The wise owner, however, concentrates on reducing costs but maintaining or increasing sales. It is possible for an operation to have a 10 percent food cost. However, what good is a low food cost percentage if there are no customers?

Looking at the statement, we cannot say that food sales dropped because of local economic conditions. Why did the sale of liquor increase? In any event, a standard cannot be determined until the cause for sales decrease has been discovered. If a 40 percent food cost was the result of elimination of theft, poor purchasing, receiving, and preparation habits, then perhaps the 40 percent food cost can be made a standard for the department. However, if a lower food cost means poorer quality food, smaller portions, higher prices, the 42 percent is a much better standard.

BAR STANDARDS

The bar figures present an interesting contrast to the food figures. As the cost of the liquor sold rose from 28 percent in January to 30 percent in February, sales volume increased from $9,000 to $10,000. Dollar-wise, this rise in sales accounts for an additional $520 contribution to gross profit. Two percent rise in liquor cost is equivalent to $200 extra cost on the basis of $10,000 sales volume. Perhaps it is wise to serve better drinks at a lower price, thereby increasing costs $200 if we can also increase gross profit $520. Only a detailed examination of the cause for sales increase can aid us in determining the proper bar cost percentage.

PAYROLL STANDARDS

The direct labor costs of the food department present no particular problem in this case. If, during the month of January, the food department could prepare and serve $32,000 worth of food with a direct labor cost of 18 percent, and if, during that time, there were no guest complaints regarding service or food, there is no reason why this department could not serve $30,000 worth at about the same percentage.

In justification of the manager's efforts, mention should be made that he evidently did reduce the dollar amount of his payroll. As sales decreased during the month of February, he reduced his payroll by $760. True, this is 20 percent of food sales. However, if he had done absolutely nothing, the payroll percentage would have been 22-1/2 percent.

This is one of the cost areas that creates a particular problem to the sophisticated operator. It *is* difficult to set a standard for *all* levels of sales. The problem of performance determination is complicated, not only because the amount of sales aids in setting equitable standards, but also because the direction of sales is a determining factor.

If sales increase, the labor cost percentage should go down, if for no other reason than the fact that all the employees in a restaurant are working at maximum productivity most of the time. On the other hand, as sales decrease, the alert operator can change time off, stagger schedules, split shifts, employ part-time help, and dismiss other employees, yet invariably if he is operating at peak sales levels, labor cost cannot decrease in identically the same proportion as sales. Consequently, if an 18 percent direct labor cost is determined as the proper performance standard for the food department, the manager will find it relatively easy to maintain this percentage if sales are moving upward and extremely difficult to maintain if sales move downward. In the first instance, with sales volume increasing, we are giving the manager undue credit for maintaining the "status quo," and in the second case not enough credit for almost perfect performance.

Ideally, with young growing operations not one, but several, performance standards should be determined for each significant change in sales volume. If the standards are determined correctly, they become a major lever for management and an invaluable aid to the owner for forecasting and budgeting future labor expense. The separation of controllable from scheduled expense and the description of each listed major sales and expense item in both dollars and percentages, provide the owner with a wealth of information for evaluating his manager's effectiveness and his restaurant's success and provide the manager with sufficient data to improve his individual performance.[1]

THE MEASUREMENT OF MANAGERIAL EFFECTIVENESS

Since the manager is responsible for every variance in sales, profit, and expense items above the line designated scheduled expenses, his overall effectiveness can be measured by the change in profits before scheduled expenses. This line shows a $750 increase in profits despite a $1,500 drop in total sales from one period to the next. Generally, because most of the expenses in a foodservice unit are fixed, semi-fixed, or semi-variable, as sales drop profits can decrease dramatically. In

---

1. The material on pp. 36-42 has been reprinted, with changes, from *How To Plan and Operate a Restaurant* by Peter Dukas (Hayden Book Company, Inc., 1973) by permission of the author and the publisher.

this instance, however, not only did profits not decrease, they actually increased by $750. Consequently, the manager should be commended for his overall performance.

Details of his performance can be evaluated by examining major revenue and major controllable expenses. For example, assuming that sales did not drop because of lowered food quality, reduced portion sizes, or poor pricing practices and that the $2,000 decrease in food sales volume was unavoidable, the manager reacted very rapidly to preserve profits. He reduced his cost of food sold 2 percent and his labor cost $760. This resulted in a gross profit after controlled expenses of $11,950 in February compared to $11,200 in January.

Part 6 — Effective Pricing Decisions

THE COMMONLY USED METHOD
TO DETERMINE SELLING PRICE

OPTIMUM CONTROL OF profits cannot be achieved until the key control points have been clearly identified and attention directed to the necessary adjustments at these points. The determination of menu prices is distinctly one of these critical areas of profit control.

Many foodservice operators determine their menu prices by multiplying the cost of food by a factor designed to produce a desired food cost percentage. For example, if the owner desires a 40 percent food cost on a menu item costing 30 cents, he will multiply the 30-cent cost by a factor of 2.5 (100% ÷ 40% = 2.5) and will set the menu price at 75 cents.

FIVE BASIC REASONS FOR NOT USING A SINGLE PRICE FACTOR

There are several good reasons for not using this pricing system. The use of a single factor for all food items:

1. Is unfair to the customer
2. Increases competition by others
3. Conceals menu items sold at a loss
4. Lowers sales volume
5. Reduces profit

If the cost of each menu item were identical, the problem of allocating all other expenses and profit equally would not exist. However, most of the menu items differ considerably in food cost. Consequently, an inexperienced attempt to multiply different food costs by the same factor cannot help but create an unfair pricing schedule.

UNFAIR PRICING PRACTICES

Consider an operation that prices a steak and a beef stew in this manner. Assuming the food cost of the steak dinner is

$1.80, and the beef stew, 60 cents, the manager desiring a 40 percent food cost, multiplies these entrees by 2.5 and sets a selling price of $4.50 for the steak and $1.50 for the stew.

Most of the operators using this pricing system do not recognize their prices are unfair to the customer. It is true that in determining the price, the cost of food is an integral part of the price. So, at a minimum, the price of the steak and beef stew must equal $1.80 and 60 cents respectively. However, when the food cost of $1.80 and 60 cents is multiplied by the same factor, 2.5, the resulting selling price of $4.50 and $1.50 creates a gross profit contribution of $2.70 from the steak customer and only 90 cents from the customer selecting the beef stew.

Assume further that in this operation net profit is 10 percent and rent expense 8 percent of sales. Why should the steak customer contribute 45 cents profit and 36 cents toward rent expense and the beef stew customer be charged only 15 cents profit and 12 cents rent?

SINGLE PRICE FACTOR SELLS MANY MENU ITEMS AT A LOSS

The other reasons for not using the single price factor are equally valid. Suppose this same operation sells ten of each menu item and has a 30 percent labor cost and a 10 percent profit, the financial statement would look like the following schedule:

		STEAK	BEEF STEW		TOTAL
Sales		45.00	15.00		60.00
40% food cost	18.00		6.00	24.00	
30% labor cost	13.50		4.50	18.00	
20% other expense	9.00		3.00	12.00	
90% total expense		40.50	13.50		54.00
10% profit		4.50	1.50		6.00

Many operations using the single price factor to determine prices would be very happy with this result—10 percent profit. However, because no direct expenses are allocated, the operator is unable to determine the amount of profit he should have obtained, or which menu item is being sold for a loss.

Assume that the pre-fabricated steak is purchased portion cut from the purveyor and that the beef stew is made on the premises with the results reported on the following page.

Most of the labor expense is evidently created in the preparation of the beef stew. Even if we speculate that 20 percent of the total labor expense of $18.00 could appropriately be allocated to the steak, the following profit and loss statement clearly shows the beef stew is being sold at a considerable loss!

	STEAK	BEEF STEW	TOTAL
Sales	45.00	15.00	60.00
40% food cost	18.00	6.00	24.00
30% labor cost	3.60	14.40	18.00
20% other expense	9.00	3.00	12.00
90% total expenses	30.60	23.40	54.00
10% profit	14.40	(8.40) loss	6.00

The use of the multiplier hides loss items in many restaurants. In this operation, only 2 menu items were utilized. The 2 items could have been 20 or 200. The essential point is that in any foodservice operation there are items that require a great deal of preparation labor such as salads, stews, chowders, pies, hamburgers, and many items such as convenience foods, frozen and dehydrated foods, boiled in bag items, milk, or ice cream that require little or no preparation labor.

OTHER REASONS FOR NOT USING SINGLE PRICING FACTOR

When no allocation of direct expenses is made to the product by the manager, there is no way he can be sure which menu items are producing profits or losses! Moreover, the failure to allocate all direct expenses to those food products that create the expense almost always results in a nonpromotive decreased sales volume and a reduced profit pricing policy.

For example, operator "A" has been promoting wine with the dinner meals. In the past he has been satisfied with a 33 percent wine cost. He wants to upgrade his wine list with imported wines that average double the cost of the domestic wine. Assume that the average cost of the domestic wine is $1.10 a bottle and sells for $3.30. How much should he charge for a bottle of imported wine costing $2.20?

It should be apparent that using the factor of 3 to obtain a selling price of $6.60 is completely noncompetitive and nonpromotive. It will not achieve the desired sales results. If the desired sales volume is not obtained, potential profits will be reduced substantially. Most of the customers will not shift from the domestic to an imported wine costing twice as much.

USE OF DIRECT EXPENSE ALLOCATION

The solution to this pricing problem is easily resolved if operator "A"remembers that an effective pricing decision can be made if all direct expenses are charged to the product creating that expense, and the remaining expenses allocated equally among two or more products. Analysis of the direct expenses of the domestic and imported wines shows "A" that aside from the cost of raw materials there are no other direct expenses.

The imported wine costs more than the domestic. This raw material purchase cost should certainly be part of the selling price. However, there are no additional direct expenses that can be charged to the imported wine. The expense of receiving, storing, issuing, and service is the same for both wines. Consequently, all other expenses should be allocated on the same equal basis to the imported wine as they are to the domestic.

Moreover, in the past, operator "A"was satisfied with the amount of profit obtained from domestic wine sales. He gained his desired profit by adding $2.20 to the $1.10 cost of the wine and selling it for $3.30. Therefore, the addition of $2.20 to the ·cost of the $2.10 imported wine determines the equitable and promotional selling price of $4.30 and produces the same amount of profit and satisfaction!

PRICE COMPETITION AND PROFITS

One of the basic reasons customers select one restaurant over another is price. When customers discover they can obtain from operation A the identical brand, quality, and amount of wine for $4.30, why should they buy the same wine for $6.60 at a similar operation? A restaurant with a 40 percent food cost and a total daily labor cost of 30% (divided as follows: 40 percent preparation, 20 percent service, 10 percent administrative, and 30 percent other) made a definite cost study of beef stew and apple pie. The study showed that the beef stew cost 46 cents and the apple pie 12 cents per portion. Management became aware that a frozen food distributor and a local baker could provide them with a portion of beef stew and apple pie at 60 cents and 15 cents respectively. These food items were equal in quality and size to the earlier ones. Management was previously selling the beef stew for $1.15 and the pie for 30 cents. What should they charge for the new items that require no preparation expense?

If they use the multiple 2.5 to obtain a 40 percent food cost, the prices will jump from $1.15 to $1.50 and from 30 cents to 40 cents. Is there a housewife who will pay these prices when she knows that she can obtain the same food value from the frozen food section of her supermarket or from her bakery for 80 and 20 cents respectively? If these products are not properly priced, sales volume and profits will be reduced considerably.

Returning to this problem of pricing, one way to determine the price is by adding the additional cost to the original selling price. The beef stew will then sell for $1.30 instead of $1.15, and the pie for 35 cents instead of 30 cents.

Although this is a much better pricing decision than the use of the multiple 2.5, it is still unfair to the customer. The guest is being charged for restaurant preparation labor that has not been utilized in the product sold. Since there are many convenience foods of all types that require very little or no preparation labor, these menu items should not bear that labor cost. Sooner or later all restaurants that have not considered this policy will find that they have priced themselves out of the market.

The chart on the facing page illustrates how the prices of beef stew and pie are determined, based first on the addition of extra purchasing expense, and secondly on the deduction of preparation labor.

The text and diagram demonstrate three methods of determining prices when a changeover is made from completely processing, preparing, and cooking menu items to purchasing these foods completely prepared. The inexperienced operator attempting to sell the beef stew for $1.50 and the apple pie for 40 cents will have a good food cost on paper, but very few sales. If a portion of apple pie costs 10 cents, it is possible to have a 5 percent food cost by pricing the pie at $2.00 a portion. The problem with this procedure is that there will be no customers!

The experienced operator who adds the cost of purchasing these items to the original cost and determines a price of $1.30

	BEEF STEW	PIE
1. Original selling price	1.15	.30
2. 30% of selling price is total labor expense	.345	.09
3. 40% of labor expense is preparation expense	.138	.036
4. Additional expense if purchased	+.14	+.04
5. Determination of price based on additional purchasing expense	1.29	.34
6. Deduction of labor preparation expense step 3	–.138	– .036
7. New price based on either step 5 minus step 6 or step 1 plus step 4 minus step 3	1.152	.304

and 35 cents is aware of the problems of overpricing but is still more considerate of himself than his customers. He includes not only the cost of preparing these items but also the same amount of profit. The forces of competition will not permit the continual excess margin of profit.

Even the frozen food distributor and the baker may begin to consider renting space and selling their products to his customers. Why should they sell beef stew to the restaurant for 60 cents and the pie for 12 cents and see the operator sell the same food to his customers for a price of $1.30 and 35 cents respectively?

One of the main reasons for the success of the specialized fast food industry is the inability of the table service industry to compete by either offering different menu items or making wiser pricing decisions.

The sophisticated operator analyzes the critical price decision points, and discovers, in this instance, that he can sell the beef stew and the pie at his original price regardless of the fact that the prepared products cost more than the processed food items.

His pricing structure enables him to continue to maintain his sales volume and his profit. In the future, because of his pricing decision he can compete more effectively to increase sales volume, to reduce preparation labor expense, to eliminate high cost or non-profit menu items, and to increase not only his probability of survival, but also his probability of profits!

GROUP PRICING METHODS

The preceding examples demonstrate how individual menu items can be priced effectively. However, except in the case of highly popular or specialty items, the process can be long and tedious. The average table service restaurant can very well consider group pricing methods.

THREE STEPS FOR EFFECTIVE GROUP PRICING

To utilize this system effectively, the menu should be analyzed and the cost of food sold divided into two groups—one group containing the cost of food sold that requires preparation labor, and the other group the cost of food sold requiring very little or no preparation labor.

The second step is to separate preparation labor from total labor expense and charge the cost of preparation labor only to the food group requiring preparation labor. The remaining labor expense, other expenses, and profit are allocated equally between the two groups.

The third step is to total each food group individually and divide the group total by the group food cost to obtain the new pricing factor.

The following example illustrates this procedure. Operator "A" averages a 40 percent food cost. Analysis of his menu indicates that 30 percent of this food cost represents items that require little or no preparation labor. Consequently, the food cost will be divided into two groups, one group containing the 30 percent that requires no preparation labor, the other group, the 70 percent that does.

"A" has a 26 percent labor cost. Forty percent of the total labor expense is preparation expense. Accordingly, 40 percent of the labor cost will be charged to the food group that requires preparation labor. The remaining labor expense, other expenses, and profit will be distributed equally among the food groups. Thus, in this instance, since the two food groups have been divided 30 and 70 percent, the remaining expenses and profit will be allocated 30 percent in one group and 70 percent in the other.

ALLOCATION OF DIRECT PREPARATION EXPENSE

		A Food group with preparation labor 70%	B Food group not re- quiring preparation 30%
		(percent)	(percent)
1. Food cost	40%	28.	12.
2. Labor expense	26%	10.4 10.92	4.68
3. Other expense	24%	16.8	7.2
4. Profit	10%	7.	3.
Total	100%	73.12	26.88
5. Current price factor	2.5	2.61	2.24

Since the total food cost of 40 percent is separated, with 70 percent in the A group requiring preparation labor and 30 percent in the B group requiring no preparation labor, 70 percent of 40 percent or 28 percent is allocated to the A food group, and 30 percent of the 40 percent or 12 percent is charged to the B group.

Forty percent of the total labor expense is direct preparation expense that is charged only to food group A. Forty percent of the 26 percent labor expense is 10.4 percent. The remaining labor expense is 15.6 percent (26—10.4). This expense must be allocated equally to Group A and B. Since Group A contains seventy percent of the total food cost and Group B, thirty percent, 10.92 percent (70% of 15.6) is allocated to Group A, and 4.68 percent (30 percent of 15.6) is allocated to Group B.

Regarding the 24 percent other expenses, 76.8 percent (70 percent of 24) is allocated to group A, and 7.2 percent (30 percent of 24) to Group B. After the 10 percent profit figure has been allocated in the same manner, each group is summed up, and the total of group A, 73.12 percent, and of group B, 26.88 percent, is determined. Finally, group A's food cost is divided into the total of 73.12 percent to obtain the price factor of 2.61. The division of group B's total of 26.88 percent by its food cost of 12 percent results in a factor of 2.24.

Operator "A" now has two price factors to help him determine prices. The cost of existing and new menu items that require extensive preparation and processing are multiplied by the factor 2.61, and the menu items not requiring this direct labor expense are multiplied by 2.24.

Section II
Planning Profits Through the Sale of Food

Part 1 — Food Cost Control

THERE ARE SEVERAL misconceptions about food cost control that are held by inexperienced operators in the foodservice industry. Perhaps these misconceptions came about because of the ease of entry into this field or because the industry is composed of over 400,000 units with a seemingly infinite variety of operations. Whatever the reason, no effective system of food cost control can be designed without eliminating erroneous judgments and gaining a detailed knowledge of the critical factors that influence food cost. Management must concern itself with a valid, reliable interpretation and evaluation of quantitative and qualitative data. Too often—because of the tremendous pressures to conform to the ideas of their peers—owners and operators as a group accept at face value and act on information that is ambiguous, and much of the time completely unreliable.

A discussion of cost control systems in general, and percentages in particular, can serve to illustrate the considerable exaggeration and misinterpretation of data that are prevalent in the industry.

COST ACCOUNTING VS. COST CONTROL

Very few operators have a cost control system, but most have a cost accounting system. The former *controls* costs, the latter *records* costs. There is considerable difference between these two objectives. Any cost control system must be developed around the administrative and operating functions that can be controlled by quantitative information. The system will pinpoint those areas in the creation of an expense that can be isolated and controlled by mathematical and other data. It will be designed specifically for the organization so that all extraneous material is eliminated; it will be practical in terms of time and in terms of cost, and it will be effective. It does what it is supposed to do: provides management with valid, reliable information to make an effective decision.

Those operators who have a system that informs management about the nature of a cost (how, when, and where it is being created), about the amount of the cost, and the variance from a budgeted or standard cost, have a cost control system. Those who do not have a system that highlights and pinpoints these areas may have an accounting system, but they certainly do not have a cost control system.

MISUSE OF PERCENTAGES

A case in point is the current misuse of a food cost percentage. Too many operators believe they have gained some magic control of food costs if they know their daily food cost or their daily food cost percentage. A knowledge of food cost or its percentage is relatively meaningless. Despite the various methods of determining a daily food cost, there is no method currently used that is accurate. Moreover, the resulting dollar or percentage figure is a blanket or an average figure. The only information it relates to the operator is that for every $100 of food sales, the food cost or the percentage might be 40 cents or 40 percent.

The food cost figure does not inform the operator whether the cost was necessary, how and where the cost was incurred, or what person, activity, food group, or menu item helped to create this expense.

Part 2 — Need for a Daily Food Cost

THE PROBLEM STEMS from the evolution of food cost control systems. Through the '20s and the early part of the '30s, the standard practice of most foodservice operators was to determine the end of the year food cost and, subsequently, relate this food cost to food sales. Beyond its other faults, this method had the major disadvantage that information was obtained too late.

BEGINNING INVENTORY METHOD

To eliminate this disadvantage, the decision was made to determine a method that would obtain daily food cost figures. The first method used to obtain a daily food cost was the inventory method. The procedure is as follows:

1. Take a beginning physical inventory	$140
2. Add total food purchases for the day	+110
3. Result: total value of food available for sale	$250
4. Subtract ending physical inventory	− 120
5. Result: cost of food consumed	$130
6. Subtract value of employee meals and other credits	− 40
7. Result: cost of food sold	$ 90

If a percentage is required, divide the $90 cost of food sold by the food sales for the day. Let us assume $225, and the result, 40 percent, is the daily food cost percentage.

DISADVANTAGES OF DAILY INVENTORY

This method of determining daily food cost has two serious disadvantages: the inventory method consumes an extraordinary amount of time and is very expensive. Each day one or two employees must take a physical inventory of the store-room, the walk-in coolers, the food in the kitchen and the dining room, and make a record of the units, brand names, sizes, weights, etc. Then, they must later submit the inventory to the office, where unit values are assigned to the food items. The values are extended by multiplying count or weight by unit value to arrive at a total unit value. Finally, all unit values are added to determine the total value of inventory.

A record has to be designed to keep track of employee meals and other credits, and a receiving record established for the value of all food received for that day. Although, this method is the most accurate determination of food costs, there are many errors that can be made that will distort the final figure.

Carelessness in taking inventory in the dry and refrigerated storage areas and in estimating value of leftovers or processed food in the kitchen; the blanket allocation of item value of sugar, condiments, and other food in the dining room; errors in pricing units, in their extensions, subtotals, and total—all contribute to the fact that unless painstaking effort and care are made, the final figure is inaccurate.

FOOD DIRECT AND STOREROOM ISSUES

Primarily because of the number of employees involved in taking and valuing a physical inventory and the time and effort consumed, a second method evolved, based on food direct to kitchen and storeroom issues. This substitute method requires adding two additional columns to the food receiving journal and installing a food requisitioning system. One column in the journal lists the value of food that will go directly to the kitchen, the other the food value that moves into dry and refrigerated storerooms. The total value of the food direct column in the receiving record, plus the total value of food requisitioned from the food stores, is the cost of food consumed for the day.

PROBLEMS OF FOOD DIRECT PLUS STOREROOM ISSUES

The food direct plus storeroom issues method of determining daily food cost eliminated the higher cost and the time and effort of employees utilized in the inventory method. However, it substituted a more complicated receiving record and required the establishment of a food requisitioning system.

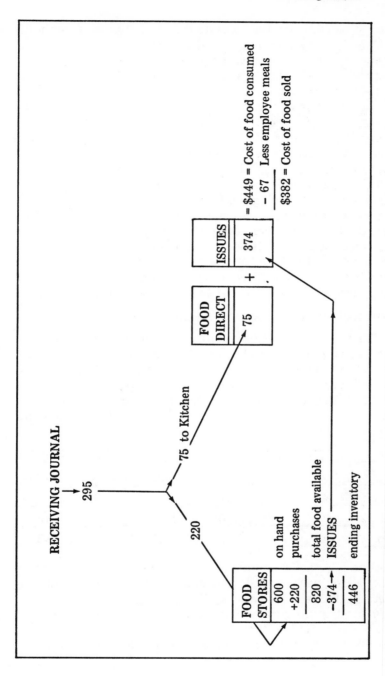

Also, it is relatively less accurate than the inventory method!

This is so because when food is sent direct to the kitchen or issued from food stores, the food value is added to the food cost for the day. However, the fact that 4 gallons of ice cream or 2 ribs were sent to the kitchen does not necessarily mean that all 4 gallons of ice cream or 2 ribs were consumed. The operation may sell only 1 gallon of ice cream and 1 rib. The remaining 3 gallons of ice cream and 1 rib are still in the kitchen. Although these items have not been consumed, they are considered an integral part of the food cost for the day.

This inaccuracy in daily food cost reporting can be partially eliminated by returning food not consumed to the dry and refrigerated storerooms and maintaining a record of food returned. Later, the value of food returned is subtracted from the daily food cost. However with the exception of limited menu or fast food operations, this return system is generally not followed, and the inventory difference creates the basically inaccurate cost figures of this food cost control system.

CUMULATIVE PURCHASE AND SALES

The third method of determining daily food cost is the cumulative purchase and sales. This method involves recording the purchases today and to-date. The total to-date purchase figure is the food cost to-date. If a percentage figure is required, the to-date purchase figure is divided by the to-date sales figure. The following simplified record illustrates this method.

	PURCHASE		SALES		PERCENTAGE	
	Today	To-date	Today	To-date	Today	To-date
Jan. 1	50		100		50	
Jan. 2	40	90	100	200	40	45
Jan. 3	50	140	125.60	325.60	40	43

Although the determination of daily food cost through cumulative purchase and sales is the least accurate, it is considerably less expensive. All that is required to obtain the daily food cost figure is to machine-add the total of the food invoices recorded in the receiving record. If a percentage is desired, merely relate this figure to food sales for the day.

SUMMARY OF DAILY FOOD COST DETERMINATION

In brief, when foodservice operators removed the disadvantage of obtaining information too late, the other major disadvantage remains: the daily food cost figure continues to be a blanket food cost. It does not tell the operator whether this amount of cost was necessary, how and where the cost was incurred, and what person, activity, or food groups helped to create this expense. Moreover, the information is relatively inaccurate, and, equally important, a daily food cost in dollars or in percentage can and does fluctuate without any employees or management cost control activity being responsible for the change. The two major factors that cause food costs to fluctuate in this way are the everyday rise and fall in sales volume (which all experienced operators are familiar with) and the sales mix.

In every operation there are low and peak sales volume days. In the more successful operations there is a minimal sales growth of 15 percent annually. As sales increase, food cost will rise, but not proportionally. Food cost is not a perfect variable expense. Consequently, a variance of 2 percent from an average can occur because the gradually increasing sales volume will create lower cost per unit with increased purchasing. Proportionally less waste, less leftover, small overproduction, and better utilization of food will result.

The sales mix described in the first section on page 13 can create an additional 5 or 6 percent increase or decrease in food cost without the use of any cost control system, without increasing either the productivity of employees or the efficiencies of the operation, and *without a change in sales volume.*

In combination, these two factors—fluctuations in sales volume and sales mix—can, if they are not understood and under control, create an 8 percent variance in daily food cost or percentage that will make any daily cost figure misleading and perhaps meaningless.

The argument for continuation of determining a daily food cost is that physical inventory can be taken at any time and that, after a few days, the fluctuations in the accumulated cost figure become less than 1 percent, and the figure is more and more accurate.

Once this decision is made, the problem becomes: which of the 3 methods of determining daily food cost, discussed to this

point, should be used? Because the beginning inventory
method is time-consuming and the most expensive, and the
cumulative purchase method the least accurate, a consensus
was reached and settled on the food direct and storeroom
issues method. This method of determining daily food cost is
currently being used by most large operations and chains.

Part 3—Other Systems of Control

COMMODITY GROUP CONTROL

BECAUSE MANY OPERATORS believe the least any practical food cost control system should accomplish is to pinpoint the food group where excessive costs are being incurred, the commodity group cost control system was established. Purchase and issues of food were separated into their respective groups: meat, fish, seafood, fruits, vegetables, and groceries. At the end of the day, the record provided the managers with a total food cost for each commodity group and a grand total of all food cost.

With this system, it is natural to assume that more effective control of food can be had by noting the fluctuations in group costs and directing attention to that group or groups whose cost totals fluctuated significantly. See the table that follows:

TABLE 3—RELATIONSHIP OF GROUP COSTS TO TOTAL SALES

Date	Meats	Poultry	Fish	$ Cost	%	Sales
1	20	20	20	60	40	150
2	30	22	20	72	44	164

PROBLEMS OF COMMODITY GROUP CONTROL SYSTEMS

Unfortunately, without a great deal more expense, time, and effort, the entire system is not only misleading, but perhaps meaningless. First, group totals will fluctuate because of seasonal fluctuations in supply. Secondly, a group total can remain steady—indicating control—yet within the food group, the cost of any one item can rise while the cost of other items is reduced. Pluses could be balanced by minuses. Also, as sales of any particular food group increase or decrease, the amount of food purchased and the cost of that food must, of necessity, increase or decrease.

A basic rule in any food cost control system is that the cost of any particular ingredient, portion, or commodity group must be related to the sales of that identical ingredient, portion, or commodity group for the information to be of any value. Neither ingredient, portion, nor group cost can be related to total sales. If this relationship occurs, the dollar figures and the subsequent percentage figures are not only meaningless but misleading.

Assume for a moment that every major flaw previously described in this system has been corrected except that group costs, instead of being related to group sales, are related to *total* sales. Assume further, for purposes of simplification, that "A" sells the food belonging to only 3 commodity groups, and that the following table is an accurate representation of the information provided by the group food cost control system.

According to "A" and other inexperienced operators, the 4 percent rise in food cost on the second of the month was caused for the most part by the significant increase in meat cost and, in a smaller measure, because of the $2.00 increase in poultry expenses. (There is nothing to worry about in the fish group—the cost remained the same.)

Aside from the fact that as sales increase, a food cost percentage should go down, even if nothing extraordinary is done by management to reduce costs, the validity of "A's" conclusions can be tested by relating group costs not only to total sales as shown in Table 3, but also to group sales as shown in Table 4 below.

TABLE 4--RELATIONSHIP OF GROUP COSTS TO GROUP SALES

	Meats			Poultry			Fish			Cost		Sales
Date	Cost	Sales	%	Cost	Sales	%	Cost	Sales	%	$	%	
1	20	45	44	20	50	40	20	55	36	60	40	150
2	30	75	40	22	50	44	20	39	51	72	44	164

Adding group sales information to group cost demonstrates how erroneous any conclusions can be if a determination is made solely by considering fluctuation in group cost. Quite obviously the total food cost rose from 40 to 44 percent because of the extremely high fish cost—51 percent—and the increase of poultry cost by 4 percent. The meat group, which operator "A" believed to be the major area of high food cost, was actually a highly profitable area. Table I had directed his attention to the wrong food groups, and the control system had broken down before it even started.

PORTION COST CONTROL

To eliminate the problem caused by a high cost item balancing out a low cost item, and to pinpoint the high cost item within the commodity group, portion cost analysis was evolved. In theory, this is a much more exact system of food cost control, since it pinpoints in the total menu the menu items that cost the most. For example, by standardizing purchasing, receiving, cooking, and serving procedures, the following facts regarding a meat entree can be formulated.

A 30-pound, oven-ready rib costs $48.00. If shrinkage after cooking is 20 percent, the 24 pounds available for sales will now cost $2.00 per pound. If a single portion is 1 pound, and a 40 percent food cost is desired, the inexperienced operator will multiply the $2.00 cost by a price factor of 2.5 and establish a selling price of $5.00 for the meat portion of this menu item.

On his standard recipe card he now believes that every time he sells his rib for $5.00 he will have a 40 percent food cost. Unfortunately, even if the costs, temperature shrinkage, and yield were identical, the 40 percent food cost he obtains in theory is not the food cost he will obtain in practice.

The reason is that a 40 percent food cost will be obtained only if *all* 24 orders are sold! If only 20 orders are sold, the rib still costs $48.00 and the revenue from this item is $100. And, the actual food cost is 48 percent instead of 40 percent!

Because most operators are not going to spend the considerable time and effort to relate portion cost to portion sales for every different portion they sell on their total menu, the system will fail before it even gets started.

SUMMARY OF COMMODITY GROUPS
AND PORTION COST CONTROL

The information on food cost control systems to this point can be summarized as follows:

Food cost, whether it is expressed in dollar or percentage amounts, is a blanket cost providing management with very little control information. The data does not tell management if that amount of food cost was necessary, what the activity was that created the food cost, which food group had the greatest cost increase, or which person was responsible. In addition to this lack of specific information, if annual or monthly figures are used, the data arrives too late for management to act. The mistakes continue to be made during the month or entire year with no corrective action taken.

The great need for daily figures, so that immediate action could be taken, resulted in the four different methods of determining daily food costs. Although timely, these figures remained a blanket cost and, in addition, on a daily basis were inaccurate.

Various cost controllers decided that on a cumulative basis the cost fluctuations caused by not taking a daily inventory would lessen, so that the inaccuracy of the daily figure would be of relatively little importance. However, the fact that the figures were still an overall food cost, and therefore uninformative, concerned many of the controllers. The commodity group and portion cost systems were developed primarily to point out the food group or the portion where the highest costs would develop.

Regarding the commodity group cost control system: if the group sales are not related to group costs, the figures are misleading. Even if this relationship is recorded, the data continues to be a blanket cost, and inaccurate on a daily basis. Also, a high cost item within a group could balance out a low cost item within the same group, uncontrollable seasonal cost fluctuations could change the group cost figure, and, finally, an increase in the commodity group total does not tell the controller which food item or items cause the cost variance.

Insofar as the portion cost control system is concerned, analysis proved that the data is inaccurate unless portion costs are related to portion sales. Although this portion cost system eliminates the cost identification problem when high cost items are balanced out by low cost items, permits adjustments of seasonal cost fluctuations, and provides identification of high cost items within a commodity group, the facts remain that the daily portion cost figure is inaccurate and a blanket cost in most respects, and that the installation and maintenance of the system is very time consuming and expensive.

OTHER FOOD COST CONTROL SYSTEMS

Both nationally known accounting firms, Harris, Kerr, Forster Company and Laventhol, Krekstein, Horwath and Horwath, have developed highly sophisticated food cost control systems for many major restaurants and foodservice chains. These systems are effective and practical for these foodservice operations.

Aside from electronic computer food cost control systems, the two systems most widely used by the Laventhol, Krekstein, Horwath and Horwath clients are the ingredient cost and the standard cost control systems.

Harris, Kerr, Forster Company is more widely known for its pre-cost, pre-control systems. Details of their food cost control systems are found in *Hotel Accounting* by Horwath and Toth, published by Ronald Press Co., and *Profitable Food and Beverage Operation* by Hayden Publishing Co.

Part 4—The Direct Profit Control System

INTRODUCTION

THE HARRIS, KERR, FORSTER and the Laventhol, Krekstein, Horwath and Horwath systems will not be analyzed in this management guide for two important reasons. First, the expense involved in installing and maintaining these systems is beyond the capacity of single unit operations achieving less than $240,000 in annual food sales, and is highly questionable for those single unit operations taking in less than $400,000 in annual food sales.

The second reason for not analyzing the more formal systems of control is that it is more relevant to discuss at this time a direct approach cost control system appropriate to the needs of the one-unit foodservice operator who achieves less than $400,000 annual food sales. Indeed, the reader may ask, is there such a system and if there is, why has it not been discussed?

This direct control approach was not introduced earlier because it could not be covered effectively or selected with conviction as the most productive system for the single unit operator, until an exploration and evaluation of *all* other alternatives were made. That has now been done. It was also necessary for the reader to recognize that the restaurant industry is composed of a vast variety of foodservice units, segmented by region, type, size, service, average check, and style of management, with a constant influx of newcomers who invariably follow one another along the same paths of control that have been used by experienced operators who have been in business longer. This automatic, unthinking "follow the others" policy should be abandoned.

An irony of the foodservice business is that as a restaurant survives and prospers, its owner will often drop the direct control he used successfully in the past and adopt the formal, expensive, indirect controls used by operators who have the larger sales volume.

VALUE OF DIRECT GROSS PROFIT CONTROL

The vital factor that must be understood in the direct control system is that the real objective of food cost control is to increase the *gross* profit figure, which is, of course, that amount of money that remains after cost of food sold has been deducted from food sales. Since gross profit is the real goal, an effective, inexpensive, direct control system, based on the many factors that cause fluctuations in gross profit, can be designed by any foodservice operator.

A thoughtful consideration of this concept should reveal that a singularly effective approach to profit control is to determine and use those factors that increase gross profit and eliminate the factors that decrease gross profit.

SIX WAYS TO INCREASE GROSS PROFIT

Basically, gross profit can be increased by the following factors:
1. An increase in the number of customers
2. An increase in the average check
3. An increase in sales volume caused by price manipulation
4. A change in the sales mix
5. A decrease in food cost
6. An *increase* in food cost

INCREASING GROSS PROFITS
THROUGH INCREASING NUMBER OF CUSTOMERS

The first section of this book proved that in any given operation achieving only a nominal volume, an increase in sales volume will produce a more than proportionate increase in profit. A simple example that follows re-proves this point. Operator "A" has a 40 percent food cost and average sales of $500 daily. His gross profit is $300. If his daily sales increase by only $50, his gross profit will increase to $330. Moreover, if a restaurant through internal and external promotion, better service, attractive atmosphere, quality food, and reasonable prices can increase the number of customers, gross profit will increase even if the food cost percentage increases!

For example, sales of $600 a day with an average food cost

of 40 percent will produce a gross profit of $360. With only an additional $100 food sales, gross profit increases $60 at 40 percent, and will increase $25 even if the food cost percentage should rise to 45 percent. Furthermore, if the manager understands that food cost is not a pure variable expense—that it will rise in dollar amounts because more food is purchased for the additional sales, but will not rise in the same proportion—then, he should also be aware that, in reality, the food cost percentage generally should decrease as sales increase, producing even more additional profit than the model suggests.

THE VALUE OF INCREASING AVERAGE CHECK

Without increasing the number of customers, sales can be increased by upping the average check per person. The average check can, of course, be increased in many ways: by combining menu items more wisely, by adding appetizers or soup at the beginning of the meal, by the addition of a dessert or beverage at the end of the meal, or by substituting wine for coffee during the meal.

Even a small addition to the average check—a 30-cent tomato or orange juice—will produce, with 500 customers and a 40 percent food cost, an additional $60 gross profit!

RELATIONSHIP OF PROFITS TO PRICE INCREASE

The earlier coverage on effective pricing (Section I, Part 6) explained in detail how manipulation of price affects profit. It should be remembered that profits can be increased by a decrease as well as an increase in price. If the decrease in price creates a better value and sales volume increases, profits will increase. A brief illustration can underline this point. Operator "A" is selling one menu item for $1.10 with a food cost of 40 percent. Thus, his gross profit is 66 cents. If he reduces the menu item to $1.00 and two customers order the item, even though his food cost changes from 40 percent to 44 percent, his gross profit is now $1.12—a profit increase of almost 80 percent.

Regarding an increase in price and its effect on profits, the only effective way to increase prices is to consider the consequences on sales volume. If the short term result of increasing prices lowers sales volume of an item, then the price increase should be reconsidered.

Only when total sales volume is maintained, or preferably increased, should this price action, or increase be continued.

WAYS TO INCREASE MENU PRICES

There are many ways to gradually increase menu prices. Very often this increase can be accomplished by substitution. For example, substitute a 12-ounce steak for a 10-ounce one. Because of the greater value, the customer will not complain. Prices should be increased on those items that create a low average check, and are in reality loss items because no allocation of preparation expense has been made. Even if customers shift completely from items that are now priced equitably, elimination of those loss items will increase gross profits.

Many times menu prices can be increased simply by changing the customer's expectations. Flaming a dessert or an appropriate entree, changing the lighting, color, or the atmosphere, shifting from bare tables to tablecloths and candlelight --even a shift from waitresses to waiters—can all increase menu prices without negatively affecting volume. A cup of coffee served by a waitress may be sold for 10 cents, but the customer who is served the same cup of coffee by a waiter expects the coffee to sell for 25 cents.

In any event, menu prices can be increased effectively if one menu item is increased at a time, if the change is gradual for the total menu, and if a check on complaints, or a check on drop in sales volume is made in the wake of a price change.

SALES MIX VS. PROFIT

The sales mix has been explained in detail on pages 13 and 14. The major points of the discussion are: since the sales or product mix in any restaurant is composed of high and low cost items, a menu is effective only when there is an appropriate balance of high and low cost items in relation to their price, and when management consistently promotes the sale of the proportionately lower cost items.

Note that this does not mean low priced items. The rule applies to *proportionately* lower cost items. It is much better to sell high cost items that carry a high price than it is to sell low cost items that carry a low price tag. The experienced owner prefers selling 10 steaks at $7.50 with a 50 percent food cost, than 20 beef stews at $1.00 with a 30 percent food cost. The gross profit from the steaks is $35.00 while the gross profit from the stew is an unimpressive $18.00!

INCREASING PROFIT BY INCREASING EXPENSES

It should be quite evident that in most instances, regardless of the factor used to increase profits, if sales are increased, the gross profit will increase. Increasing food cost is no exception to this rule. However, sales are very rarely increased if the additional food cost represents poor purchasing practices, theft of food, overproduction, waste, and other similar causes. Under these circumstances, the rising food expense, instead of adding additional food value on the plate and thereby promoting sales, tells an owner that his management has very poor control of food expense. The result of the rising cost of food sold under these circumstances is an immediate, proportionate decrease in gross profit.

On the other hand, a deliberate, controlled increase of food expense designed to promote and increase sales by giving the customer additional food value invariably increases profit. There are many examples of the effective use of this principle throughout the industry.

A Brown Derby shifts from plating a salad in the kitchen to informing customers that they can make their own salads—as much as they want—from the attractive salad bar in the dining room. Other examples of this kind of effective promotion are: Wolfie's in Miami, which offers a free basket of miniature Danish rolls for breakfast and free Kosher pickles for lunch or dinner; the Four Seasons in New York City with its Crepes Suzette dish flamed with Grand Marnier; the Pontchartrain Hotel in New Orleans, which offers a foot high, foot long Baked Alaska; and the various bars all over the country that increase their beer and liquor sales with free crackers, peanuts, pretzels, or cheese spreads.

HOW TO INCREASE PROFITS BY DECREASING EXPENSES

Whenever cost of food sold is decreased without decreasing the food value offered to the customer, profit from food sales will increase immediately and in exact proportion to the cost reduction. Because expense reduction creates the additional profit immediately, this method remains the most widely used approach to increase profit.

Unfortunately, as noted in the earlier description of this approach, sole reliance on quantitative information to reduce expenses has 4 major flaws:

1. The emphasis is on cost reduction, not gross profit increase; *this distinction is vital.*

2. The total daily figure is usually inaccurate and occasionally misleading and very seldom informs management whether the amount was necessary, who was responsible, or in which activity the increased expense occurred.

3. The installation and continued maintenance of a cost system based on gathering, evaluating, interpreting, and using data is very expensive, perhaps prohibitive for the low volume food sales operator with low sales volume.

4. The data approach is indirect, not direct. The information will tell the operator that a cost variance occurred, but it does not control the expense. Other approaches can control the expense before or as it is being incurred.

Consequently, there are not any remaining options. The restaurant manager is faced with the challenge to *reduce cost of food sold and at the same time to maintain or increase his food sales.*

Once the dual nature of the problem is accepted, the direct approach to gross profit control is relatively easy to use effectively. The manager understands that gross profit can be increased immediately by determining the factors that create an increase in food expense, without a corresponding increase in sales, and eliminating all of those factors from the operation. Since the maximum increase in gross profit is attained by eliminating *every one* of these factors, the information should be organized to facilitate this result. The total operation should be subdivided by activity and each functional area studied to determine and isolate those factors that decrease sales volume or increase food expense without a corresponding increase in food sales. In most restaurants, these activities include menu planning, purchasing, receiving, storing, issuing, processing, serving, selling, and controlling.

MENU AND PROFIT MANAGEMENT

Regarding menu planning: too many operators fail to realize that this production and sales blueprint is one of the most important implements they have to operate their unit profitably. In terms of production and sales promotion, a carefully designed menu not only determines the amount, type, and variety of food items to be purchased, received, stored, issued, prepared, processed, and served, but also the type, size, and amount of equipment required to serve these respective items. Careful planning of the menu determines the square feet, volume, and allocation of space required in the kitchen and service area and, additionally, the price of each item, the average check, the seat turnover, the type of customer, the volume of business, the amount of investment, and the potential profits!

Since sales volume and the relationship of menu price to menu cost is so important for profit control, a menu—the basic merchandising tool of a restaurant- should be designed to increase sales volume and to increase profit. A simple, essential truth that must not be forgotten!

Before the operator lists his various menu items, he should consider and eliminate those factors that increase cost of food sold without a corresponding increase in food sales.

MENU PLANNING

In the planning of the menu, the following factors must be considered:

1. *The demand for the menu item.* Sales increase, and the business succeeds, to the extent that the business matches the food values it offers with the food values desired by its customers.

2. *The availability of the item*, first in the storeroom, then the market. In an instance where a particular menu item is in short supply, an appropriate substitute may be purchased.

3. *Potential tie-in* with holidays and special events. Food sales can be increased substantially if special menus are designed for Easter, Valentine's Day, festivals, parades, conventions, and other special days and events that interest and involve the general public.

4. *The merchandising appeal of the plate.* Give some serious thought to the psychological impact that the food on the plate makes when the customer first sees it. Food can appeal to all the senses by providing a variety of colors, textures, shapes, temperatures, and contour.

5. *The number of entrees* on the menu. Should the menu be limited or extensive? The decision is important not only

because of the increased possibilities for waste and theft, but also because at some point the enlarged menu increases both payroll expense and investment in production equipment.

6. *The production requirements* in the kitchen. Consider the present skills of employees and the different kinds of equipment in the kitchen so that the work load is equitably distributed among the employees and the equipment. Select menu items that fully utilize present skills and equipment without requiring additional employee training or equipment.

7. *Selling price of each menu item* should be determined so that customer values and sales volume are maximized. (See Part 6 of Section I on effective pricing.)

8. *The resulting sales and cost mix* should be studied so that gross profit is increased and is pre-determined. If an analysis indicates a high rate of high cost items in relation to their selling price, make appropriate substitutions, if warranted, *before* the menu is offered to a guest.

9. *The design and format of the menu* should be planned so it is completely understandable unpredictable, and highly promotional. The use of esoteric terms is a serious mistake for most foodservice operations. The customer will not select items if he does not know what he is buying. A menu that is completely predictable is dull and monotonous. Finally, create an effectively designed menu for the specific operation—consider shape of the menu, colors, style and size of print, menu item grouping for easy selection, and effective use of blank spaces.

FACTORS IN PURCHASING

Leaving the important area of menu planning, let us consider the equally important factors in purchasing that contribute to any effective direct gross profit control system. To succinctly state these factors:

1. *There should be centralization of purchasing power and responsibility.* If two men are responsible, then neither is accountable.

2. *Separation of purchasing and receiving.* In any operation, if one employee is purchasing, a different employee in another department should receive.

3. *Individualized purchase specifications.* Purchase specifications that are copied from competitors, trade magazines, or books have very little merit. Food must be purchased to pro-

vide the best grade, weight, or count in relation to its cost, its planned use, and its selling price in the specific operation. If a restaurant sells 2 eggs for 65 cents, the owner will probably purchase medium or large eggs. If he receives $1.65 for two eggs, he should purchase extra large or jumbo. Also, if he plans to use celery for soup, he should specify stock celery, but if he plans to use celery as an appetizer (for example with cream cheese), he should specify a fancy grade.

4. *No speculative purchasing!* If a purchasing executive can increase profits by purchasing six months or a year in advance, he should leave the restaurant industry and become a trader in the commodity exchange. There is a great deal more potential for earning money speculating on the exchange than in the restaurant business.

5. *There must be a cost budget for food purchases.* The easiest way to tie up money in food inventory, and promote waste, spoilage, and theft is to allow the purchasing agent to buy as much as he wants from whomever he wishes to purchase.

6. *There must be a purchase record.* The purchasing agent must be held accountable for his purchases in the areas of type, quality, weight, count, grade, and price. Without a written record, accountability is impossible, and without a copy to the receiving man, there can be no comparison with what was ordered and what was received.

7. *There must be an audit of purchasing and receiving records or invoices and subsequent payments.*

THE RECEIVING FUNCTION

The following points regarding the receiving function should be kept in mind (they are self-explanatory and require no comments):

1. *Check on receiving methods and procedures.*
2. *Provide adequate facilities and equipment.*
3. *Check on costs, weight, quantity or grade.*
4. *Store perishable foods as soon as possible.*
5. *Keep record of goods received.*
6. *Establish system of obtaining credit for damaged goods or food not received.*
7. *Guard against theft by receiving man.* Theft in the receiving area has two dimensions that must be controlled: agreements made by trucker and purveyor to defraud, and

stealing by the receiver. No food item should be received unless a copy of the detailed purchase order is available. The copy serves as an authorization to receive and permits comparison with the invoice. Discrepancies between the invoice and the purchase order are noted and changes made on the invoice at that time. The corrected invoice and purchase order are sent to the office for posting. A spot physical inventory check at any time will reveal shortages.

THE STORAGE AND ISSUE FUNCTION

Regarding the next function, storage and issue, keep these simple but important points in mind:

1. *No divided responsibility.* Only one employee should be responsible for receiving, storing, and issuing.

2. *Food should be properly placed in storage areas.* Food, such as eggs and milk, should be kept off the floor; any food with a high fat content should not be stored near fish, cheese, or food products with a strong odor.

3. *Foods should not be stored at wrong temperatures or humidity.*

4. *Make daily inspection of storage areas.*

5. *There must be good sanitation.*

6. *Insist on frequent reports on slow moving or dead stock inventory.*

7. *There should be a physical or perpetual inventory.*

8. *No careless pricing of issues!*

9. *There should be a record of food authorized and issued from the storeroom.*

THE PREPARATION AND PRODUCTION FUNCTION

These brief reminders about the preparation and production function should be noted:

1. *Avoid excessive trim of vegetables and meats.*

2. *Make sure there is adequate mechanical equipment for boning, slicing, cutting, trimming, carving, and peeling.*

3. *Check on net yields!*

4. *Make use of end products.*

5. *Provide standard recipes.*

6. *Make sure correct methods of cooking are used.*

7. *Have foods cooked at correct temperature to preserve quality and yield.*

8. *Do not let foods be cooked too long.*

9. *Do not cook too much. Avoid overproduction by not cooking too much.*

10. *Cook in small batches where possible, to preserve quality.*

11. *Plan precise scheduling of food production.*

12. *Avoid inadequate, faulty, or dirty equipment.*

THE SERVICE FUNCTION

Pay attention to these points about the service function:

1. *There should be strict control or record of food served or leaving the kitchen.*

2. *Maintain standards for portion sizes.*

3. *Provide uniforms.*

4. *See that leftovers are properly taken care of.*

5. *Be sure foods are served promptly to the customer.*

6. *See that customers are given personal service.*

7. *Carefully train your service personnel.*

8. *Provide adequate supervision.*

THE SALES FUNCTION

Here are some factors to consider regarding the sales function:

1. *Keep a tight control on theft by sales personnel.* To increase tips, a waitress or waiter might serve a larger portion, a double order, or a steak to a favorite customer and write "hamburger" on the check. Watch this! Also, if money is given to sales personnel, waiters' checks can "conveniently" disappear.

2. *Control cashier theft.* All waiter checks should be tinted and numbered for control purposes. The tint prevents erasures or changes in the check. Missing checks can be discovered early if all waiters' checks are placed in consecutive numerical order. Checks should also be examined for improper pricing and totaling. An occasional surprise cash register reading can help prevent theft from the customer or from the business. Any significant cash overage or cash shortage is immediately suspect.

3. *Keep your eyes open to avoid "walk-outs."*

4. *Provide a sales history.* A menu copy can easily become a sales history by recording number of items sold and other pertinent data. This could provide management with a popularity index, a guide for purchasing and production, and a means of detecting total and menu item sales trends.

5. *Avoid unattractive food, inadequately served in a negative atomosphere.*

6. *Insist on good internal and external promotion.*

THE CONTROL FUNCTION

Finally, some significant points to remember about the control function:

1. *There should be a check on, and a division of, responsibility.* A cashier, for example, should not have a register reading key. The employee who has the register reading key should not count the cashier's cash.

2. *Do everything you can to avoid inadequate, disorganized, insufficient, or misleading factual information.*

3. *Make a forecast of sales or expense budget.*

4. *Use systematic procedures and policies for purposes of control.*

5. *Audit your daily food sales and expenses.* Depending on the size and complexity of the foodservice unit, all, or a selection, of the following records could be used:

  a. A complete sales history
  b. A physical and perpetual inventory
  c. A duplicate, numbered purchase order form
  d. A receiving record
  e. An accounts payable ledger
  f. A cash and check disbursement journal
  g. Tinted, numbered waiters' checks
  h. A pre-check machine, food checker's report or a duplicate checking system
  i. Register tapes and control keys for reading
  j. Reconciliation records of cash disbursed at any activity that has cash transactions
  k. A record of employee and officer meals
  l. A record of voided checks

SUMMARY OF DIRECT GROSS PROFIT CONTROL

To summarize the main points developed in the direct gross profit control system:

1. The entire focus of this system is to use any factor that will increase gross profit and to identify and eliminate all factors that reduce gross profit.

2. Since increasing sales volume (by increasing the number of customers, manipulating menu prices, or increasing the

average check) increases gross profit, management must analyze all related factors and use them to create the desired result.

3. The sales and cost mix of each menu should be studied and corrected to increase gross profit *before* the menu is offered to the customers.

4. The gross profits can be immediately increased by manipulation of cost of food sold. Profits can be increased by increasing food expense if the increased expense provides more food value for the customer, and by decreasing food expense if the decreased expense represents the elimination of waste, theft, poor management decisions, and lack of control.

5. No expense should be reduced and no management decision should be implemented if the net result is a material decrease in sales volume.

Section III
How To Build Profits
Through Payroll Control

Part 1 — Labor Cost Control

INTRODUCTION

ONE OF THE MOST important issues, and perhaps the most vexing, facing the owner of today's (and tomorrow's) food-service operation is the cost of personnel. In discussions with many industry leaders, the consensus is that there does not appear to be a single mitigating factor now—or in the future— that will materially decrease labor cost.

In fact, the trend to shorter work weeks, increased fringe benefits, longer vacation periods, growth of unionism, steady continual increase in minimum wages, increased demand for employees, and competition by other industries for labor, are all factors that dissuade the intelligent owner from a belief that the serious problems of personnel and labor cost will resolve themselves.

By 1985, the continual annual increase in food sales of $2-1/2 billion will create a $75 billion industry requiring 5 million employees at a $3.00 plus minimum hourly wage.

If more emphasis is not placed on automation, labor saving equipment, increased use of new food technology, better food production and service methods, or a wiser investment in methods, materials, services, and systems to control labor expense, most of the nation's food and lodging operations will be in considerable trouble.

THREE MISCONCEPTIONS REGARDING PAYROLL CONTROL

Many foodservice owners and managers believe an effective cost control system can be based on the relationship between labor cost and sales volume. There is merit in attaching importance to this relationship. However, this consideration is only one of the many approaches toward control of payroll costs. The manager who relies solely or mainly on this approach cannot really control his labor cost, because he misunderstands the nature of this tool. There are three *major misconceptions* that should be reviewed here:

1. Labor expense can be controlled if the manager obtains an accurate weekly total of labor expense as a percentage of sales and compares his expenses with the percentage of the preceding week.

2. The only way labor expense can be controlled is by setting up a system of reporting and analyzing the payroll dollar.

3. Labor expense can be controlled by combining the two approaches above, and by adding a detailed information system that will pinpoint the activity and cause of a higher labor cost variance.

MISUSE OF WEEKLY LABOR COST DATA

Consider the first misconception: the bleak record of business failures testifies that reliance on weekly labor cost data to control payroll expense disregards the important fact that a weekly labor cost is very uninformative, that it is an average of the week's labor cost, and that it does not consider the many daily factors that can create significant fluctuations in expense.

Regardless of the fact that the weekly labor cost figure is accurate or that it is expressed as a dollar or percentage, the data does not tell management on what day or during which meal period a high labor cost was incurred, or in what activity or how the additional expense was created, *or* who was responsible for creating the additional expense.

Also, many managers tend to forget that a weekly labor expense is an average. The very human tendency to assume everything is fine when one week's labor cost is the same—or almost the same—as the preceding week, will cause the loss of many labor saving opportunities.

In any operation, because of daily sales fluctuations, even though the dollar amount stays the same, the labor cost percentage will fluctuate significantly. For example, it is very possible to have a 40 percent labor expense one day, a 20 percent another day, and an average of 30 percent for the two days or for the week. The manager who is satisfied with the 30 percent weekly labor expense *averaged*, may be relatively unaware that in terms of sales productivity, his labor expenses *doubled* during the period when labor expense rose to 40 percent, *or* that if he had acted quickly—through better scheduling, days off, no overtime, or extra help—he could have maintained the high productivity of 20 percent throughout the week. On the basis of $6,000 weekly sales, this savings, a $600 immediate addition to gross profit every week, is created solely by more effective labor cost control.

THE SECOND MISCONCEPTION

The second misconception about labor expense control relies on a system of gathering and evaluating the payroll dollar in order to control labor expenses. This procedure is misleading and ineffective on two counts. First, as shown in the example in the preceding paragraph, although the dollar amount stayed the same during the week, the labor cost fluctuation of 20 to 40 percent demonstrated potential labor savings of $600. Management needs both the dollar *and* the percentage figures to analyze data and to effect savings.

USE OF MAN-HOUR APPROACH

More important, although many managers are familiar with, and use, the dollar-spent approach properly to control labor, too many do not use (or ineffectively use) the number of standard employees approach. The dollar-spent approach is a measure of the cost of labor; the standard employee approach is a measure of their productivity. One is a dollar-spent view; the other is a man-hour productivity view.

The failure to use *both* approaches to control labor is extremely unfortunate. The man-hour approach is as important as the dollar-spent approach. For example, assume that two similar restaurants, A and B, have a $30,000 monthly sales volume and both have a 30 percent labor expense of $9,000. Is restaurant A as efficient as restaurant B. . .?

Not necessarily! Suppose that restaurant A required 50 standard employees to generate its sales volume while restaurant B required only 25 employees to generate the same sales volume. Restaurant B is obviously twice as efficient as restaurant A even though total payroll expense is identical.

MONTHLY SALES AND THE STANDARD EMPLOYEE

The results of a management study of over 80 profitable foodservice operations, ranging from deluxe table service restaurants and cafeterias to coffee shops and fast food operations, demonstrated that, as a general rule, regardless of type of operation, the most successful and profitable units were generating a minimum of $1,000 monthly sales for every standard employee in their pay.

There were differences in man-hour productivity. For example, several of the extremely well-run operations, especially in the fast food segment of the industry, were generating $1,700 to $1,900 monthly sales volume for every standard employee. Some relatively profitable table service restaurants and cafeterias were as low as $500 to $600 per standard employee. This variance in sales productivity was caused, not only by differences in managerial skills, but also, by the difference in type of foodservice operation, and the region where the unit was located. For example, contrast the number of people needed to operate a table service restaurant with the number required to man a McDonald's. Also, the number of employees hired in any operation is influenced by location; it may be in a low wage, high unemployment area or in a region which is highly unionized with a short supply of skilled employees.

THE STANDARD EMPLOYEE AS A
GENERAL GUIDE FOR CONTROL

Despite these differences, however, a sound rule can be formulated that any well-run foodservice operation should not have more than one standard employee for every $1,000 monthly sales. A standard employee is the equivalent of 40 man-hours a week. If an employee works 40 hours a week, he is a standard employee. If he works sixty hours a week, he is 1-1/2 standard employees. If two part-time employees work twenty hours each a week, they are one standard employee.

The number of standard employees in any operation is determined by averaging the total weekly man-hours worked in any two or more test weeks (excluding the manager's hours) and dividing by forty.

Extra help, part-time help, overtime—all man-hours except the manager's—are included in the total. If the monthly sales figure of any operation falls to $600 or lower, immediate attention should be given to determining the reason for the low man-hour productivity.

THE THIRD MISCONCEPTION

The third misconception about labor expense control, the combining of the prior two misconceptions and the adding of a detailed information system that will pinpoint the activity and the cause of the higher labor cost variance, is equally ineffective in controlling labor cost for two basic reasons. The first reason involves the cost of the system. The detailed quantitative information that is necessary to establish administrative control, to prepare operating budgets, to provide proper distribution and control of expenses, and to provide an accurate reporting of income is expensive to install and to maintain. Obviously, the potential savings and control afforded by the system must be equal or greater than the cost of the system. In many operations doing less than $150,000 annual sales volume, this may not be the case.

Part 2 — Is This Work Necessary?

BEFORE *ANY* LABOR cost control system is installed or details of the system implemented, the owner or manager should study each unit of work in the operation and decide *whether work is necessary.*

PRODUCTIVITY AND EXAMPLES OF JOB ANALYSIS

The basis and subsequent effectiveness of any labor cost control system is focused on the vital question, is this work necessary? *Before* the operator recruits and selects better qualified employees; *before* he installs more efficient supervisory procedures, analyzes his schedule to determine days off, split shifts, or incorporates a staggered system of arrivals; *before* he implements better motivational techniques to make his employees more productive; *before* he does anything, he must examine every department, every activity and ask himself, *is this necessary?*

A detailed job analysis of all activities will help the owner answer the question, "Why am I having this work done?" Several years ago, a consultant studied the Kennedy Airport Airline-feeding facility for two weeks. He noted that the layout of equipment was all wrong: employees were spending more time walking than working; they were using only one hand to fill the tray because they were holding the tray with the other hand; and the trucks were taking close to an hour and a quarter to load a flight. He changed the layout, showed the employees how to use both hands, and set up a truck arrival and departure schedule. These changes reduced the labor force from 83 to 51 employees.

Another chain operation had 6 restaurants. For twenty

years each operation had an assistant food cost controller, several food pre-preparation people, a meat cutter and his assistant, and equipment such as potato peelers and power meat saws. An intensive study proved to the owners that centralizing the food cost control function and setting up a central commissary in one of the larger restaurants, would not only eliminate the need for a cost controller, pre-preparation employees, meat cutters, and related equipment *in each place*, but also provide increased savings through larger purchase orders delivered to one place, and increase the unit manager's control and effectiveness in ordering from the commissary.

TWO MAJOR APPROACHES FOR PAYROLL COST CONTROL

Any food or lodging operation can reduce its labor expense significantly *if* both the payroll dollar and the man-hour approach are used, and *if* the question is always asked, "Is this work really necessary?" Begin with the more important or more costly work areas for larger payroll benefits. Each activity should be carefully analyzed.

1. What is the purpose of the job? It is not enough to say that the purpose is to cook the food or to punch a hole. The purpose should be investigated in detail because it may not be useful. The food may be purchased cooked, or the hole may not be necessary.

Why must the work be done within the operation? Could the entire value or parts of the job be purchased from an outside source? Can the elements of the work be separated and distributed to other employees? Can a subsequent or prior operation eliminate the need for this operation? Can this operation be eliminated by changing the order of processing, the size, shape, form, and nature of the work, or by acquiring new materials, labor-saving equipment, or inventories?

Question every detail with an open mind. Do not be like Commodore Vanderbilt. When George Westinghouse approached the New York Central's Vanderbilt about the Westinghouse air brake, the Commodore is said to have chided his receptionist, "I have no time to listen to fools who believe they can stop a train by blowing air on wheels."

2. If the job is necessary, divide the operations into elements and see if an element can be eliminated, combined, or the work simplified. Simplifying a job does not need the talents of a time and motion engineer, but rather the applica-

tion of an alert mind using the guidelines listed below.
- Analyze each element or motion. Why is it necessary?
- How long does the operation take? Why?
- Are materials moved a minimum distance with no back-tracking?
- Should the sequence be changed?
- Is there a productive material flow-plan being used?
- Are both hands idle at the same time? Or is only one hand idle? Why?
- Can momentum be employed to assist the work?
- Does the sequence permit an easy and natural rhythm to the work?
- Are definite and fixed stations provided for all tools and materials?
- Are these as close as possible to the worker. Could tools, equipment, work stations be pre-positioned in a semi-circle in front of worker?
- Can chutes, slides, drops, or gravity be used?
- Can it be put on wheels?
- Can an automatic-feed or conveyors be used?
- Can it be processed by a different machine?
- Is present equipment operating at correct temperatures and speed?
- Can a holding device be used to free both hands?
- Can the travel distance be shortened?
- Is one worker using a superior method that could be used by others?
- Can rehandling or recounting be avoided?
- Can the work be done earlier or later during slow periods?

VALUE OF JOB DESCRIPTION AND JOB SPECIFICATION

Once the determination has been made that a job is necessary, the greater portion of the job analysis has been accomplished, and work can begin on a job description and job specifications. The detailed job description involves a planned sequence of the task, its key points, the materials, and the procedures and equipment that should be used. The subsequent job specifications note the various characteristics needed by an employee to perform the work satisfactorily. These forms are invaluable aids to management. In combination the job analysis, description, and specifications provide the following:

The elimination or reduction of unnecessary work

Improved productive effort

A forecast of manpower requirements

A basis for much more intelligent recruiting, selection, training, and scheduling of employees

The establishment of the economic value of the job and the basis for an organized method of overall wage and salary determinations

Trained supervisors and improved supervision

Assistance in placement, transfers, and promotion

Uniform procedures for performance

A basis for systematic control of payroll costs

FOURTEEN BASIC REASONS FOR HIGH PAYROLL EXPENSE

There are fourteen fundamental reasons for high labor costs:

1. *Failure to combine dollar and man-hour approaches to control labor expense.* Both approaches are needed.

2. *Dependence on weekly or monthly labor cost figures.* The information is received too late and is meaningless because it is an average cost over a period.

3. *Use of cost figures that are uninformative.* A $300 expense, even if it were reported on a daily basis, does not in itself inform management where, how, at what meal period, or who was responsible for the $300 expense.

4. *Failure to use both dollar and percentage of sales data* to analyze and control expense. The dollar expense may remain the same or the payroll expense increase, yet analysis can demonstrate that considerable savings would be effected because of a proportionately greater sales volume.

5. *Failure to provide job analysis, description, or specifications* means that there is no elimination of unnecessary work or elements of work, no improvement of the work that is necessary, no forecast of manpower requirements.

6. *Failure to obtain a sufficient number of applicants for the position open.* The best selection program fails unless a sufficiently large number of persons apply for each job.

7. *Poor selection of employees.* A sick organization that is plagued by incompetent, unproductive employees—where hostility, self-interest, absenteeism, high turnover are rampant —is not going to control its labor expense by firing the employees. The same people who hired the old employees may very well select the new employees in the same old image.

New procedures for evaluation and selection must be planned. The sophisticated interviewer notes every detail of each applicant and relates these observations to the specifications for the job. He plans the informal or formal interview, designs an application form that will add to the specific information he has obtained through his observation, schedules an interview free from interruptions, puts the applicant at ease, selects the best qualified man, considering both the short and long term consequences of the selection.[1]

8. *Inadequate orientation, training, and motivating of employees.* Production will go down and labor cost increase whenever employees are placed in a working environment that depersonalizes them, minimizes their personal needs, makes them feel unimportant, or does not effectively train and develop them. One of the major indictments and paradoxes of business is that it will spend a considerable amount of money to select a productive employee, then throw him in the working environment with a "sink or swim" attitude.

New or inexperienced employees should never be put to work without a thorough orientation and detailed instruction. They should be made to feel welcome, important, and an integral part of the organization.[2]

9. *Inadequate, incompetent supervision.* Top management may create the environment and the policies that can aid employees as a group which functions effectively. However, in the final analysis the individual employee's degree of job interest, job satisfaction, and effective performance depends primarily on his immediate supervisor. Supervision is a difficult task. For some who are unable to change their negative attitudes and behavior, who are unable to observe, listen, and communicate effectively, it is an impossible task. Effective supervision eliminates poor working habits, provides better trained, more cooperative and productive employees, utilizes better work scheduling, and helps create for each individual employee a physical and psychological environment that develops the employee as an individual and unites him/her with a cohesive, enduring, productive employee team.

10. *Impulsive, unplanned hiring and consequent overstaffing.* Too often in many of the larger operations, because of

---

1. Peter Dukas. *How to Plan and Operate a Restaurant,* rev. 2nd ed. (Hayden Book Co., 1973), Chapters 12 and 13.
2. Ibid.

seasonal peaks or increased peak periods, extra or part-time help is hired and when the busy period is over, the additional employees are retained. This type of hiring and overstaffing can be prevented very simply by considering each necessary job as a single unit having its own particular work schedule, by naming and numbering each position, and by making it a rule that no new employee can be hired unless a numbered position is open or the manager approves.

11. *Lack of labor saving equipment.* Many competent authorities agree that in general an owner can invest $2,500 on any equipment that will save one hour of labor a day. Not only will well-considered purchases of equipment reduce labor expense, but equally important, the equipment is never late, never argues, does not steal, and does not require fringe benefits such as health and life insurance, vacations with pay, pensions, or payroll taxes. Any employer who prefers that his dining room employees walk sixty feet to check on a food order instead of installing signal lights or walkie-talkies, that his kitchen employees work with faulty conventional equipment instead of new, improved equipment, or with three sinks instead of a dishwasher, that an employee cut salad or peel potatoes instead of providing a salad maker or a potato peeler is not really interested in the welfare of his employees or the reduction of labor expense.

12. *Poor layout of equipment.* An efficient layout not only decreases payroll expense by eliminating costly over-handling, processing, and transportation, but also increases the efficiency and ease with which the work is performed. Two of the most important principles involve the sequence of handling food and the frequency with which each piece of equipment is used. The work should flow in a straight line from receiving to the customer, and the equipment that is used most frequently should be positioned in front of, or as near as possible to, the employee. When these two principles are utilized properly, the elimination of employee motion results in considerably increased production and significantly lower payroll costs.

13. *A poorly designed and extensive menu.* Aside from fluctuations in labor expense created by changes in sales volume or sales mix, payroll expense is significantly increased by the number of menu items and their nature. Since the menu is a list of items to be processed, the first major decision

in designing an effective menu is to determine the number of entrees that will be listed. This decision will affect the sales volume and the expense of producing the items.

The larger menu will need more people, employees with greater skills, as well as different equipment to produce the items. By eliminating menu items with a low popularity index and streamlining the menu, the wise manager may eliminate much of the special equipment, and eventually one or more positions.

14. *No insight in using sales, scheduling, performance standards, and other payroll data to materially reduce the payroll expense.*

Many foodservice operators know the effect that fluctuating sales volume has on payroll expense. The problem, however, is to discover what caused the increase or decrease in labor cost. Have wage rates been increased during this period? Was the change in fixed or variable labor expense? How many were on vacation or vacation relief? Have service and sales been improved because of the payroll increase? Was the staff at minimum or maximum productivity? Were labor saving changes made during this period?

The effect that sales fluctuations, sales mix, pricing decisions, and break-even points have on labor cost has been described in the general cost control section of this text. The remaining information is discussed in the parts that follow.

An actual application is contained in the following anecdote.

THE MANAGER'S DESK was littered with papers—food, labor cost sheets, profit and loss statements, and the like. His worried face relaxed for a moment with recognition as I walked into the office.

"Say, you're just the man I want to see." He gestured, "Have a seat."

"What's the trouble?" I smiled sympathetically.

"Everything's the trouble. This past month, except for my salary, I haven't made a cent profit. I've been going over these all morning," he pointed at the papers, "and I can't see any way to reduce costs." He paused, then, "What would it cost to hire a good foodservice consultant?"

I answered, "About $15,000 to $25,000 a year."

"Be reasonable," he demanded. "I don't average more than $20,000 sales a month."

"O.K.," I responded, "let's talk seriously. You could have him by the day for about $20,000 or give him a percentage of the increased profits, or a combination of salary and percentage."

He shook his head. "I can't afford that."

"Sometimes you can't afford not to do it," I answered. "A competent analyst can see things which you cannot because you're surrounded daily with hundreds of other problems—problems pertaining to personnel, service, promotion—in addition to problems pertaining to costs. Let me give you an example. Select a department which you think is operating profitably and I'll see if I can reduce that department's costs."

He looked at me defensively. "Why should I select a department if I think that it is operating profitably?"

"Very simple," I answered, *"because if you think the department is operating profitably you have probably done little or no thinking about it."*

He stared at me for several minutes, then turned to the desk, selected a paper and handed it to me. "I'll call your bluff," he said. "That's the bakery's departmental cost and sales monthly breakdown sheet.

"In that department, my labor cost is 19 percent, my food cost 42 percent, and my profit is $408.00 a month. You take it from there."

I studied the department and noted the following items:

Sales.	$1,200
Cost of food sold . . .	$504.00
Payroll expense.	228.00
Accrued gas expense. . .	60.00
Total allocated expenses	792
Gross profit	$ 408

"What kind and how many items do you sell daily?" I asked.

"You don't catch me there," he laughed. "I sell on an average 30 pies, 6 cuts to a pie; 4 cakes, 12 cuts to each cake; $5 to $6 worth of rolls a day at 3 cents a roll. On a monthly basis, I'll sell about 900 pies, 120 cakes, and $175.00 worth of rolls."

I did some rapid figuring.

	Pies	Cakes
No. of item sales. . .	900	120
No. of cuts per item	6	12
	5,400	240
		120
Total cuts available	5,400	1,440
Price per cut. . . .	.15	.15
	27000	7200
	5400	1440
Sales per item. . . .	$810.00	$216.00

Pies. . . .	$810
Cakes. . .	216
Rolls. . .	175
Total sales	$1,201

His figures were surprisingly accurate.

I thought for a moment; then, lifted the phone and called four bakeries. They quoted an average price of 55 cents for a 9-inch pie, 65 cents for 9-inch layer cake, and for sweet rolls 18 cents a dozen.

Picking up the pencil again, I began to work.

	Pies	Cakes	Rolls (doz.)
No. of items needed. .	900	120	486
Cost per item . . .	.55	.65	.18
	4500	600	3888
	4500	720	486
Purch. price of items	$495.00	$78.00	$87.48
Cakes. . .	78.00		
Rolls . . .	87.48		
Total cost of items	$ 660.48		
Total revenue	1200.00		
Gross profit	539.52		
Previous gross month profit. . .	408.00		
Increase in profit	131.52		
No. months in year	12		
	26304		
	13152		
Increase in profit per year. . .	$1,578.24		

The manager studied the figures. "There must be something wrong," he pleaded. "Where's the catch?"

"There is no catch," I answered. "You have eliminated your payroll and gas expenses by purchasing the items instead of baking them on your premises. While the cost of the purchased food is higher than your present food cost, it is less than your present total allocated expenses. In point of fact, however, the food cost is still high. If you decide to purchase these pies, you should shift to seven cuts per pie. The pie you will be buying has a 9-inch diameter and you were previously using 8-inch pies. Here, let me show you."

No. of cuts needed to produce identical revenue. . .	5400
No. of pies to purchase 5400/7 or.	772
Cost per pie	.55
Total pie cost	$ 424.00
Cost of cakes	78.00
Cost of rolls.	87.48
Total cost.	589.48
Total revenue.	1200.00
Gross profit per month. . . .	610.52
Previous monthly profit. . . .	408.00
Increase in profit monthly. .	202.52
No. of months in year	12
	$2430.24

He looked at the figures unbelievingly. "Say," he said finally, "how about looking at this departmental report."

I smiled and rose from my seat. "Come on, let's get that dinner you promised me."[1]

---

1. Courtesy of Room Service Management.

Part 3—How to Reduce
Payroll Expense

SEVENTEEN RULES THAT WILL REDUCE PAYROLL EXPENSES

IN ATTEMPTING TO reduce labor costs, the controller cannot begin by haphazardly attacking a particular cost that seems important at the time. A labor cost control system *consists of an organized, planned, frontal attack on all of the previously listed causes for high cost.* These are the summary rules to reduce payroll expenses:

1. Use both payroll dollar and man-hour productivity data.

2. Obtain information that is timely; if possible, yesterday's payroll and a forecast of tomorrow's.

3. Obtain data that is accurate, informative, and usable. If the information is inaccurate, does not answer your "why, where, when, how the cost was incurred questions," the data is useless.

4. Use both dollar and percentage figures in the analysis.

5. Examine each job, activity, and element of a job to see if it is really necessary.

6. For every separate activity, make a detailed job analysis, job description, and job specification.

7. Determine methods to increase the number of applicants for any position opening.

8. Improve selection of new employees by utilizing unbiased personal observations, written application forms, job specification sheets, and by planning the interview.

9. Improve the orientation, training, and motivation of new and experienced employees.

10. Create a basic manning table. This will inform management of the number of positions needed at varying volumes of sales.

   a. Personally check your assistants, supervisors, and department heads. Dismiss the incompetent. Do not follow the line of least resistance and dismiss the untrained, insecure employee. The same unproductive, untrained labor force will evolve again if there is the same leadership that created the problem in the first place.

b. Ask the competent supervisors to fill out cards on each job within their department indicating the jobs that are necessary to the operation and the employees that are most capable of filling these jobs.

c. Consider each job as a single unit having its own particular work schedule and area or station.

d. Name and number each necessary job.

e. Make it a rule that new employees can be hired only if one of the numbered positions is open.

f. Determine minimum and maximum wage levels for each position.

g. For control and budget purposes, classify and identify each job within a department. Payroll cost breakdown can be accomplished in many ways depending on the size and type of operation. A departmental classification of jobs may be done by listing your employees under the section or department in which they work. For example, under *Receiving, Storing, and Issuing*, receiving clerk, other receiving help; under *Preparation*, vegetable cleaners, salad preparation workers, butchers, et al.; under *Processing*, cooks and bakers; *Service*, counter girls, waitresses, busboys, and head waiters; *Junior Administrative*, bookkeeper, office help, cashiers, food checkers; and under *Administrative*, manager, day assistant manager, night manager, and food production supervisor.

h. Determine fixed and variable positions within each department. A fixed position is one that must be filled regardless of decrease in sales volume; a variable position is one that can be eliminated if sales decrease.

i. Organize your executive control through people occupying fixed positions.

j. Determine production and/or performance standards for all variable positions. How many customers should be served per waitress? How many sales per cashier? How many covers per dishwasher?

k. Assemble performance standards in table form to show number of employees needed for various volumes of work.

l. Check to see that the number of employees needed in any one department is not based only on peak load requirements.

11. Analyze menu offerings. Check the number of items offered, and the balance of high and low cost items; check popularity index of menu items and convenience foods.

12. Purchase labor-saving equipment.

13. Invest in obtaining greater quantity of raw materials, light equipment, etc., for the purpose of lengthening the time period required by labor. If a given volume of work must be done in a shorter time, more employees will be needed.

14. Check space arrangement and layout of equipment.

15. Schedules:

a. *Position or Station Schedules* A schedule of employees should list name and station of work for each day. This is used by the employees in an operation that rotates workers to different stations, and by management to check how effectively each station is covered during the day and under varying volumes of sales.

b. *Hour Schedules* This is the common type of schedule used in many operations. It is composed of a list of employee names and their respective hours of work during each day of the week. Unless this schedule has incorporated enough payroll statistics so that cost per man-hour can be related to sales per man-hour, it will have no value except to the employee.

c. *Wage Schedule* On this type of schedule the first row contains a list of the employee names classified according to the departments in which they work. The second row contains a list of their daily wage rates or hourly wage rates if they are part-time workers. The succeeding seven rows (if this is a seven-day operation) are headed by the days of the week. Each row represents and contains the total daily wage of each employee for that day. If this wage schedule is used in conjunction with a daily sales figure, management will be able not only to judge the relative productivity of labor per day—that is, compare cost of labor to sales for each day—but also to check labor productivity by departmental standards and, if necessary, determine cost per man-hour with sales per man-hour.

Where proportionally large increases of labor cost occur because of slow days or slack periods within any one day, days-off and reliefs can be adjusted on the work schedules, or part-time (and occasionally full-time) workers can be dismissed to make labor more productive.

16. Actively use sales, scheduling, performance standards, and other data. The data and information should be studied and used. Put the improvement into effect. If the information is not used, then it is not needed.

17. Follow through. Continuously check to see that the improvement stays in effect. Most employees will slip back into their old methods unless they are required to use the new idea, procedure, or method constantly.

PAYROLL PRE-COST CONTROL

Several restaurant operators have added the pre-cost concept to steps outlined above. They have evolved a system for their operation to forecast their sales volume and, on the basis of the sales forecast, forecast their costs for that period.

1. On the basis of past sales records and general and local economic conditions, forecast your sales by months one year in advance.

2. The week before the month becomes current, divide the month into weekly forecasts.

3. Refine your next week's forecast by considering unusual local events, holidays, weather, and other special items that may affect next week's business.

4. Set up a standard payroll budget for each department in your operation for one month in advance.

5. On the basis of your next week's sales forecast, refine that week's payroll budget and set up a system of weekly and daily reporting of payroll cost by each department.

6. Compare actual costs with budgeted costs. Any excess beyond budgeted costs requires a detailed explanation. The excess represents the amount of money that might have been saved if each department had stayed within its budget.

7. Find out when and why each excessive cost fluctuation occurred. The cost may have occurred because of overtime

hours, hiring of part-time employees or extras to replace those on vacation or those absent for the day. Or the excess costs may have occurred because the operation stayed open too long or the number of employees needed was determined by peak load requirements. Whatever the reason, when you eliminate the cause, you will eliminate the cost.

Many restaurant operators may feel that the pre-cost pre-control system cannot be followed and that it is too much work. But every day these same managers or owners must spend money for food and labor. The reason is that they anticipate sales. The reason they spend a certain *amount of* money for food or labor is that they forecast a certain amount of sales. Since a forecast of sales and cost is made one way or the other in any operation, it is obviously better to design a detailed, organized system of forecasting based on actual sales and cost records than to depend on intuition or a hunch.

The rules described above can decrease the labor costs and increase the profits of any foodservice operation because they eliminate the basic causes of high payroll costs. To make these rules effective, remember that an idea or improvement is useless unless it is *used*. Also, there must be complete follow-through.

PEAK LOAD ANALYSIS

For example, one cause of high labor cost may be that the number of employees required was based on peak loads. This cause, like the others, should be analyzed, checked to see if it applies to your own operation, and followed through until that particular cause of high labor cost is eliminated.

To illustrate the analysis and application of this idea, consider a restaurant that has its peak period at lunch. During this period, 12:00 to 1:30, it serves 225 customers. From 1:30 until 2:00 it serves 25 customers. At two o'clock this restaurant closes for three hours—it opens for a small dinner business that begins at five o'clock.

The idea that the number of employees required in any department should not be determined solely on peak loads can be illustrated in any department that contains variable positions—the service department (waiters, waitresses, busboys), the preparation department, and the cooking department. As an example, we will select the dishwashing department.

Since the restaurant serves 225 people in an hour and a half, it will serve, on an average, 75 customers every half hour during its peak period. If this same operation averages 6 dishes per customer, the dishwashing department will clean 75 times 6, or 450 dishes every half hour.

Looking at our investment requirements, if we bought about 8 dozen of each dish item, we would have based our investment in china on peak loads. This in turn means that we must have enough dishwashing employees to supply our guests with clean dishes, glasses, and silverware at the rate of 450 for every half hour, because a little after the first half hour we will be out of clean dishes.

With this situation we will probably need three dishwashing employees: one to scrape and pre-flush dirty dishes, one to stack and load the machine, and one to remove clean dishes, stack on clean dish table, and transport clean dishes to the area of use. Moreover, if we purchased a machine capable of washing 450 items of china, silver, and glassware every half hour, the three dishwashers would be through with their work about two o'clock, and we would have to put them to work doing something else.

However, if we increased our investment in dishes and glassware from 8 to 15 dozen of each item, we could buy a smaller machine and base our labor requirements on the total operating period instead of peak load period. The peak load is 225 customers from 12:00 to 1:30 and 25 customers from 1:30 to 2:00. Consequently from 12:00 to 5:00, we would have to take care of 250 customers times 6 items per customer or 1,500 items. Since we may want to give the operator time to change the tank water, clean out the dishwashing machine, and prepare for the evening peak period, we might want him to be through by 4:00 with the dishwashing. This gives us four hours—from 12:00 to 4:00—to wash 1,500 items, or about 375 items per hour. On an average, a 20x20 rack holds 25 items, and since 375 items divided by 25 is 15, the capacity of the machine should be about 15 to 20 racks per hour. But one operator can certainly handle 15 to 20 racks per hour. Therefore, we not only can save by purchasing a smaller dishwashing machine but also eliminate at least one dishwasher.

One successful restaurant operator in California solved a similar problem without the mathematics outlined here. He had 6 dishwashers who were being paid $2.00 an hour or a total of $480 a week. The dishwashers were usually through at 2:30, and the manager had to run around finding something for them to do.

When he got tired of doing this, he dismissed one dishwashing employee. The dishwashers were now getting through with their work about 3:00. The manager reflected on this situation and decided to dismiss another dishwasher and raise the remaining employees' wages $.10 an hour. The dishwashers were getting through with their work around 3:40. The manager finally decided to make one of the remaining four dishwashers the head dishwasher, give him a raise of $.20 an hour, dismiss another dishwasher, and increase the pay of the remaining two dishwashers another $.10 an hour. The head dishwasher was now paid $2.30 an hour and the two dishwashers, $2.20 an hour. Their total wage for a 40-hour week was $268, a savings of over $212 a week, or $11,024 annually!

There are, of course, many better approaches to labor cost control than the one described in the preceding paragraphs. Making management decisions on the basis of personal observation is useful but limited. An approach using quantitative data is not only more informative, but also more productive in terms of control, and more useful as a means of developing managers.

USE OF HOUR AND POSITION SCHEDULES

The hour and position schedules described earlier are utilized rather extensively by the industry, either as a written form or as oral instructions. The major use of these schedules is to provide the employees with information about hours of work, time off, and stations they will cover. Management uses these schedules to ensure adequate coverage during peak periods and to control the number of employees on duty on any one day.

These schedules can also be used constructively to lower payroll expense by analyzing and comparing performance standards for the particular *group* of employees with the *number* of employees. In one operation that had employed 18 waitresses in 2 dining rooms and one cocktail lounge, the number of waitresses was reduced to 12 by determining peak sales periods, proper days off, and by utilizing a staggered system of arrivals so that waitresses were on duty when they were needed.

A study of that operation's past sales records revealed that Saturday was the highest peak volume day of the week; Sunday and Friday were next highest respectively; Wednesday and Thursday were next; Tuesday's volume consistently averaged less than Wednesday and Thursday. And Monday was generally the lowest sales volume of the week. On the analysis form these days were numbered 1 to 6, 1 indicating the busiest day, 6 the slowest day.

In terms of guests in the dining rooms and the cocktail lounge, the hourly cash register readings indicated that the busiest period on any day was between 5 and 9 p.m., the second busiest period was between 12 and 3 p.m., and the slow period was between 6 and 8 a.m.

A study of the sales volume per hour and the number of guests on the busiest day demonstrated that at any one time, 2 waitresses were needed between 6 a.m. and 8 a.m., 4 between 8 a.m. and 12 p.m., 7 between 12 p.m. and 3 p.m., 5 between 3 p.m. and 5 p.m., 8 between 5 p.m. and 9 p.m., and 5 waitresses between 9 p.m. and 1 a.m. A similar study was made for the other days. The completed waitress requirements are shown on the "Analysis—Number of Persons Per Key Hours" chart.

ANALYSIS—NUMBER OF PERSONS PER KEY HOURS						
	3 Fri.	1 Sat.	2 Sun.	6 Mon.	5 Tues.	4 Wed.	4 Thur.
Slow period	2, 6-8 3, 8-12	2, 6-8 4, 8-12	2, 6-8 3, 8-12	2, 6-8 3, 8-12	2, 6-8 3, 8-12	2, 6-8 3, 8-12	2, 6-8 3, 8-12
Second busiest	6, 12-3 4, 3-5	7, 12-3 5, 3-5	6, 12-3 4, 3-5	5, 12-3 3, 3-5	5, 12-3 3, 3-5	5, 12-3 3, 3-5	5, 12-3 3, 3-5
Busiest hours	8, 5-9 5, 9-1	8, 5-9 5, 9-1	8, 5-9 5, 9-1	6, 5-9 4, 9-1	6, 5-9 4, 9-1	7, 5-9 5, 9-1	7, 5-9 5, 9-1

Because the owner of the restaurant did not believe loyalty and productivity could be encouraged with part-time help or with service employees working a split shift, all waitresses were put on a 6-day schedule, 9 hours a day. (The 9-hour day included 1 hour for rest periods and a meal.)

Accordingly, the schedule (p. 106) of the busiest day incorporates the owner's wishes and the information provided by the analysis of number of persons per key hours.

The analysis of the number of persons per shift per day and the subsequent position schedule are constructed both from the information shown on the schedule of the busiest day and

NUMBER OF WAITRESSES ON DUTY SATURDAY, PER KEY HOURS AND PER SHIFT

Waitress Identification	A.M. 6	7	8	9	10	11	12	2nd busiest hours 1	2	3	4	P.M. 5	6	busiest hours 7	8	9	10	11	12
1																			
2																			
3																			
4																			
5																			
6																			
7																			
8																			
9																			
10																			
11																			
12																			

NUMBER OF WAITRESSES DAILY AND EACH PERIOD

	7	8	10	1	4	7	10
Saturday	2	2	4	7	5	8	5
Friday & Sunday	2	2	3	6	4	8	5
Wednesday & Thursday	2	2	3	5	3	7	5
Monday & Tuesday	2	2	3	5	3	6	4

from the allocation of days-off during the slower sales volume days.

Note that only 12 waitresses are now required instead of 18, a payroll savings of almost $300 weekly. Morale, service, and productivity have been improved. Not only can waitresses make more tips because there are fewer waitresses, but also they are less bored because, on the low volume days or as the sales volume drops during the day, there are fewer waitresses on the floor.

Service is improved becasue, as sales volume increases on an hourly basis or on a daily basis, more waitresses are automatically scheduled.

WAITRESS SCHEDULE

Position number	Name	Fri.	Sat.	Sun.	Mon.	Tues.	Wed.	Thurs.
1	C.L.	5-1	5-1	5-1	off	5-1	5-1	5-1
20	S.R.	5-1	5-1	5-1	5-1	off	5-1	5-1
21	S.R.	5-1	5-1	5-1	5-1 #1	5-1 #20	off 21	5-1
22	S.R.	8-5	8-5	8-5	5-1	5-1	5-1	off
23	S.R.	12.9	12.9	12.9	12-9	12-9	off	12-9
24	S.R.	6-3	8-5	off	6-3	8-5	8-5	8-5
25	S.R.	#DR 6-3	6-3	6-3	off	6-3	6-3	6-3
30	D.R.	5-1	5-1	5-1	off	5-1	5-1	5-1
31	D.R.	5-1	5-1	5-1	5-1	off	5-1	5-1
32	D.R.	off	6-3	6-3	6-3	6-3	6-3	6-3
33	D.R.	12-9	12-9	12-9	8-5	off	12-9	12-9
34	D.R.	12-9	12-9	12.9	12-9	12-9	12-9	off

ANALYSIS—NUMBER OF PERSONS PER SHIFT PER DAY

	Fri.	Sat.	Sun.	Mon.	Tues.	Wed.	Thurs.
	2,6-3	2,6-3	2,6-3	2,6-3	2,63	2,6-3	2,6-3
	1,8-5	2,8-5	1,8-5	1,8-5	1,8-5	1,8-5	1,8-5
	3,12-9	3,12-9	3,12-9	2,12-9	2,12-9	2,12-9	2,12-9
	5,5-1	5,5-1	5,5-1	4,5-1	4,5-1	5,5-1	5.5-1
No. waitresses per day	11	12	11	9	9	10	10

USE OF WAGE AND SALES ANALYSIS

To eliminate the misleading information provided by an average, and to provide detailed daily and departmental psyroll information, a wage-sales schedule can be used effectively for any operation. Earlier, it was pointed out that the typical weekly labor cost figure or percentage is relatively useless. This figure is not only misleading, but, more to the point, like a food cost percentage, it is a figure that—even if accurate—does not inform management whether that amount of labor expense is necessary, where the expense occurred, or how the expense was created. Moreover, the weekly labor cost figure is an average. On any one or two days having high-volume sales, a labor cost percentage can be 16 percent and during slow days can rise to 32 percent. At the end of the week, the average payroll expense represents 24 percent of sales and the manager will not even be aware that, had he scheduled employees properly, he could have saved an amount equal to 10 percent of sales.

A combined wage and sales schedule can be used to pinpoint the problem days and can, after evaluation of the causes for high labor expense, lead to a considerable expense reduction. The typical weekly wage and sales schedule can also be analyzed on a daily and hourly basis. See schedule below.

Although the weekly labor cost is slightly over 24 percent, the schedule pinpoints the fact that during the last four days

	Mon.	Tues.	Wed.	Thurs.	Fri.	Sat.	Sun.	Total
Receiving Dept.								
R. Adams	$12.00							
F. Cesak	8.00							
Dept. Total	$20.00							
Other Depts.								

Total Labor Expense	$210	179	200	191	191	191	191	1,353
Sales	$700	640	800	830	870	850	829	5,519
Percent Labor Expense	30%	28%	25%	23%	22%	22.5%	23%	24.5%

TABLE 5—CONTROL AND LABOR COSTS

Time	7:00	8:00	9:00	10:00	11:00	12:00	1:00	2:00	3:00	4:00	5:00	Total
Receiving												
R. Adams		$1.50	1.50	1.50	1.50	1.50	1.50	1.50	1.50			
F. Cecak				$1.00	1.00	1.00	1.00	1.00	1.00	1.00	1.00	
Dept. Total		$1.50	1.50	2.50	2.50	2.50	2.50	2.50	2.50	1.00	1.00	20.00
Other Depts.												
Labor Expense	$12.00	14.00	16.00	16.00	16.00	34.00	26.00	28.00	12.00	12.00	30.00	216.00
Sales	$20.00	45.00	35.00	20.00	45.00	110.00	130.00	100.00	20.00	35.00	160.00	720.00
Percent Labor Expense	60%	31%	46%	80%	36%	30%	20%	28%	60%	34%	18%	30%

of the week—because of higher labor productivity and better utilization of employees—labor cost is actually below 24 percent. However, at the beginning of the week, labor cost rose to 30 percent, resulting in the elimination of a potential savings of 7 percent of sales. The schedule can also provide detailed information on departmental labor expense and departmental sales productivity.

Assuming that the manager wishes to analyze Monday in more detail, the schedule can easily be redesigned to provide information on an hourly and peak-period level by substituting the day columns with hourly columns, the day's wages of each employee with hourly wages, and the sales figure with hourly sales figures. Note the wide variation in hourly sales productivity and hourly labor expense in the table on page 109.

Section IV
Profitable Bar Management

Part 1 — Evolution of Bar Management and the Repeal of Prohibition

A NEW ERA IS INAUGURATED

DURING THE ERA of Prohibition, the foodservice industry had to be content to provide good quality food at economical prices. With the repeal of Prohibition in 1933, however, the elements of competition gradually forced the restaurateur to supplement his food sales with the sale of liquor.

In the beginning many operators made this change, not to add to their total income, but to retain the customers who desired a cocktail before dinner or an alcoholic beverage afterwards. The restaurateurs soon discovered that through sale of liquor they not only kept their customers, but they also added an important source of additional revenue. A new era was inaugurated.

BASIC PROBLEMS OF LIQUOR CONTROL

The change brought a number of new headaches. Management was forced to learn thoroughly the business of selling liquor. There were problems in accounting for costs and profits; deciding on item and quantity purchasing; determining minimum and maximum inventory levels; installing productive methods and controls in receiving, storing, and issuing; hiring honest, efficient personnel to serve liquor; standardizing amount and mixture of liquor in straight and mixed drinks; pricing effectively; and meeting the challenges in tying the sale of liquor to the sale of food.

The solution to these varied problems evolved from the painstaking methods of trial and error—the occurrence of an incident and the application of a remedy. Some of these vexations, such as the accounting of liquor and payroll costs, were readily solved because of their similarity to other problems in the past. Other difficulties, such as effective purchasing and pricing, were solved gradually. A few problems, such as elimination of theft or control of costs, were, in many respects, never solved. Because of varying environmental factors, each operator installed his own method of theft prevention and cost control, which was never uniform and seldom completely effective.

The important fact is that the control of liquor sales should be much easier than the control of food sales. This is so because liquor is not perishable, and, more to the point, because the quantity and quality of each bottle is *always* the same.

However, with the exception of major chains that can afford expensive systems of control, most bar and cocktail lounge owners have been unable to maximize their profits and minimize their waste and theft. Because their volume of liquor sales cannot support and maintain a detailed control system, they attempt to control through a system that haphazardly attacks each problem as it arises or through personal observation.

Obviously, an owner attempting to maximize profits and eliminate theft and excessive expense with personal observation or by reaction to random problems, will fall far short of his goal. Optimum control can be achieved only when all the critical points are identified and a profit center developed that automatically, in most instances, prevents theft or losses; and when—through management attention and action—the necessary adjustments are made at these points to maximize profits.

Part 2—A Basic Liquor Control System

BASIC LIQUOR CONTROLS

AN EASY WAY to visualize the necessary total control is to take the position of an observer looking down from the apex into the interior of a pyramid. The pyramid has three horizontal levels. The top level is the smallest and contains the control center. The bottom level, along the base of the pyramid, is by far the largest and contains the employees, quantities of liquor, and money. If no lines of control flow from the control center at the top, conditions in the base will be chaotic.

With no management of activity and no assignment of responsibility, employees mill around from one area to another. They are not only unproductive, but also are actually colliding with, interfering with, and obstructing the activity of one another. There is neither direct controlled flow of liquor to a customer nor money to the control center. To the observer at the apex of the pyramid, everything seems to be aimlessly moving around in completely erratic circles. And it is.

FOUR BASIC STEPS FOR BETTER CONTROL

In order to survive and prosper, the first order of business is to determine the critical activities, consider their basic similarities, and, for general control purposes, combine those activities that are similar. (In small bar operations the activities can be combined into three broad areas of control: management and administration, receiving and storage, production and sales.)

The second order of business is to assign duties and responsibility for a designated activity to each employee and to direct his individual actions.

The third order of business is to radiate control lines from the profit center to each critical point. These controls can be used in any bar or cocktail lounge, even though more complex systems have been installed. In this way, these inexpensive management controls can be effected through a combination of paper forms, policy decisions, and a method of checks and balances that can operate throughout the system.

Returning to our pyramid: an additional control step would be to install a *formal* liquor cost control system on the *second* level of the pyramid.

The primary order of business demands that these critical activities be controlled: purchasing and paying for liquor, receiving, storing and issuing, production and sales. To simplify and pinpoint controls on personnel, let us say that the following 6 employees are hired: an accountant, a purchasing agent, a storeroom man responsible for receiving, storing, and issuing liquor, a bartender, a cashier, and a waiter.

CONTROL OF PURCHASING

Because of the regional uniformity of liquor prices, an important aspect of purchasing control is the proper determination of minimum and maximum inventory levels and *not* the cost of individual liquor items. Generally, the cost of any particular brand of liquor is pertinent to merchandising. When liquor dealers have offered promotional deals on a particular brand, it is advisable to purchase that brand in quantity for use as bar liquor.

On the other hand, the excess diversion of cash into inventory results in an immediate reduction of working capital, a subsequent impairment of credit, and possible loss of physical item control. An excessive inventory increases paper work and probability of theft, creates storage problems, and is no guarantee that the particular liquor item asked for by the patron is in stock.

For these reasons, competent operators require that their purchasing people buy only up to a certain percentage—generally a maximum of 40 percent of estimated weekly sales—or insist that they purchase according to well-defined inventory levels.

No set figures can be given for the various inventory levels because of the differences in item and total sales of each individual operation. However, an analysis of liquor sales checks will reveal which items move slowly, which quickly, their seasonal activity, and the maximum sales volume of each item. For the most part, maximum inventory levels are set for those liquor items that are not in great demand, and both maximum *and* minimum levels are set for those items that are more popular. The minimum inventory level of each item is determined by an analysis of its highest sales volume for the period between ordering and receiving the liquor. The maximum level is fixed by determining 1-1/2 times the sales volume of each brand between one delivery date and the next.

Since there are too many operations that have paid for goods that were never ordered and/or never received, the cardinal rule for control of this function is: a purchasing agent should not be responsible for receiving any goods that he purchased, nor should he certify or authorize payment. These are 3 separate functions, and in this system 3 different people are made responsible: the first to purchase, the second to receive, and the third to pay.

When the purchasing person places a liquor order, a duplicate purchasing order form must be provided to systematically record all the pertinent information. The printed form (Figure 1) is headed with the firm's name and address and is num-

FIGURE 1—PURCHASE ORDER FORM

	Gordon-System, Inc. 712 W. 54 Street		Purchase Order No._____ Date_____	
Quantity Ordered	Size	Item		Price
Remarks:				
Received by:_____ Purchased by:_____				

bered serially to account for each order. Space is provided to record the date, the seller's name and phone number, a complete description of the goods that are to be received, remarks or instructions concerning the items, the validating signature, and the signature of the employee who receives the goods.

The purchase order form serves not only as a *record of responsibility* but also as *an authorization to receive.* The standing policy regarding this form is that no liquor can be received unless the size, number, brand, and unit and total cost on the invoice is exactly as recorded on the purchase order form. The original purchase order is sent to the accounting office and is inserted in a folder entitled "Liquor Ordered." The carbon is forwarded to the storeroom man who will receive the liquor.

RECEIVING, STORING, AND ISSUING

Receiving, storing, and issuing should be the sole responsibility of one employee. Like a cashier in a bank who cannot add to his individual bank unless he receives a written deposit, or subtract from his bank unless he receives a written check, all of the storeroom man's activities and actions are limited, recorded, and completely controlled.

When delivery is made, the storeroom man checks the bill against the copy of the purchase order form for discrepancies. He checks weight, quantity, size, and price, inspects the cases for physical damage, and accepts delivery.

As soon as the liquor is safely stored, the storeroom man will bring his perpetual inventory cards up to date, sign the duplicate purchase order form—thus indicating that he has received the items—and attach the order form to the bill. Later he will send them to the accounting office.

The accounting staff then checks the bill against the original purchase order, inserts the duplicate purchase order form in a folder entitled "Liquor Received," records the bill in the purchase journal, and brings the office perpetual liquor inventory up to date.

From the time that the liquor is delivered until it is sold, the responsibility for control of costs rests mainly with the storeroom controller. Although authority must be delegated to him commensurate with his responsibility, that authority is limited, clearly defined, and subject to checks and balances.

He cannot receive any liquor without a purchase order form,

and he cannot make an authorized withdrawal of liquor without a beverage requisition slip. He should be given the only key to the liquor storeroom so that he is solely responsible for all liquor in the storeroom.

In general, his duties—if they are commensurate with a controller's responsibilities—are to receive, store, and issue liquor; systematically record all changes in inventory; gather, classify, evaluate, and interpret all data regarding consumption of liquor; present in writing a comprehensive analysis of liquor costs; point out any discrepancies between consumption and sales of liquor; and indicate the method by which losses may be eliminated.

Most of his working hours are concentrated therefore on the task of collecting and interpreting information for management. To aid him in amassing the detailed data systematically and properly, there must be forms that record sufficient information on which to base corrective measures and that are practical enough not to interfere with other employees' work routines. These basic liquor forms and detailed liquor cost records are described fully in the pages that follow, as the cost control analysis of the various functions of liquor merchandising is developed.

The perpetual liquor inventory forms (Figure 2 on p. 120) that were mentioned earlier are simply a series of printed cards cataloged according to type of liquor and filed alphabetically according to brand name. Each inventory card should indicate the name of the brand, its size and cost, the order level for the purchasing of the liquor, the maximum and minimum inventory levels, the current dealer's name, the date that the liquor was received and issued, and the balance on hand.

The use of the perpetual inventory cards eliminates the need for bin cards and provides the liquor cost controller with detailed information concerning every brand of liquor in the storeroom. In addition to the specific cost data, a periodic analysis of these cards will show *for each brand* the number of bottles purchased and issued from the storeroom, the balance of inventory, the inventory turnover, and whether or not the inventory levels and order point determination are correct.

CONTROL OF STORAGE, PAR STOCK, AND ISSUING

Aside from the specific properties of certain liquors, such as sparkling wines where temperature, position, and humidity

FIGURE 2—PERPETUAL INVENTORY CARD

Dealer_____		Order Point __24__		Brand_____					
Case Price _____		Max. Inv.__72__							
Unit Price_____		Min. Inv.__12__		Size__ Qt.					

Date	Rec.	Issued	Bal.	Date	Rec.	Issued	Bal.	Date	Rec.	Issued	Bal.
1/1			34	1/10		7	59				
1/2		6	28								
1/3		7	21								
1/5		6	15								
1/7		5	10								
1/8	60	4	66								

are factors, the storage function involves primarily the ease with which items can be moved in and out, as well as the *safety* of the liquor.

A comprehensive inventory can be taken very quickly if the types of liquor, such as rye, scotch, and gin, are shelved separately. The more popular brands within each group should be readily accessible on the lower shelves, and the less popular brands should be shelved in the least accessible area. Usually there is no need to shelve the liquor alphabetically; however, if the owner desires, each shelf can be labeled with the name and quantity of the liquor.

The liquor storeroom should have only one entrance, which is kept locked except for those times when the liquor cost controller enters for business reasons. He should be made entirely responsible for the safety of the liquor during the storage period. In order to place this responsibility for inventory shortages directly on him, he should have the only available key to the liquor room. In case the original key is lost, the liquor cost controller should seal a duplicate key in an envelope identified as "liquor key," write the date and his signature on the envelope, and place it in the office safe.

The control of liquor issues is based on a constant par stock level and proper procedures fixing the responsibility of liquor moving to the bar. The head bartender should be responsible for initiating these activities. He begins his task by determining the quantity of each brand he needs for daily business and permanently fixes the location of each bottle behind the bar. The other bartenders are instructed to return the bottle to its designated space after each drink is served. The exact placement of each bottle not only conserves the time and motion of the individual bartender and enables him to serve his customers quickly and effortlessly, but also aids in the taking of the weekly or monthly physical inventory and in training a new bartender.

Next, the head bartender determines the number of bottles that will go into the display or bar storage areas—this quantity is usually another day's supply. These liquor items are grouped according to type of liquor and stored in the locked bar storage or display areas. The number of bottles in the serving area plus the number of bottles in the storage and display areas comprise his par stock.

As the bottles of liquor from the serving area are emptied, the head bartender replenishes his supply from the bar storage areas. At the close of the day's work, or in the morning before the bar is open for business, he lists the empties on a triplicate requisition form and affixes his signature. The liquor cost controller checks the number and brand of empty bottles against the requisition, then issues full bottles for replacement. Consequently, the head bartender is responsible for the liquor at the bar, for maintaining a par stock, and for initiating the function of issuing.

The liquor or bar requisition (Figure 3 on p. 122) is a printed form in triplicate recording the number of the requisition and the date; the number, size, and brand of liquor requisitioned; and three signatures—that of the authorized employee who requisitions the items, that of the storeman who checked the empties and issued the liquor, and that of the bartender who received the liquor.

One copy of the bar requisition is kept by the head bartender so that he has a written record of all the items he ordered and received for any one day. The second copy is held by the liquor cost controller so that he can adjust his perpetual inventory cards and show the authorization for the decrease in inventory.

After the liquor is received and the bar requisition signed by the head bartender, the original form is sent directly to the accounting office so the office staff can make an adjustment in the office perpetual liquor inventory record. This original

FIGURE 3--BAR REQUISITION

Date_____		BAR REQUISITION	A407
No.	Size	Brand	
Requisitioned by_____ Issued by_____Rec'd. by_____			

requisition form is kept as part of the authorized liquor requisitions and issues, and it is compared with the copies when any discrepancies in perpetual or physical inventories occur.

SUMMARY OF CONTROLS IN THE PURCHASING AND PAYMENT OF LIQUOR

Remember these points about the function of the purchasing agent.

1. He cannot indiscriminately purchase any brand, size, or amount of liquor from any purveyor at any price.

2. He is not authorized to make payment or to authorize payment of a liquor invoice.

3. He cannot receive liquor.

Thus, the purchasing agent's power is clearly defined and limited. The owner or manager sets maximum and minimum inventory levels for every brand of liquor. No invoice will be paid unless it is accompanied by a written, numbered purchase order in duplicate. The purchasing agent must provide management with a detailed record of every purchase for which he is held strictly accountable. Finally, since he cannot make payment or receive liquor, there are no loopholes and no opportunities for embezzling or conspiring with purveyors to make fraudulent purchases.

Under these conditions, theft or embezzlment can occur only if the purchasing agent joins forces with two other employees, in two different departments, each of whom have separate controls imposed upon them: the storeroom man, who is the only person responsible for the liquor when it is received, stored, and issued; and the accountant, who is solely responsible for the reconciliation of invoice, purchase order, liquor-received journal, and the stock ledger, and who must provide management with all supporting documents before the manager will make payment.

SUMMARY OF RECEIVING, STORING, AND ISSUING

This summation of the receiving, storing, and issuing function should be kept in mind:

1. The storeroom employee's authority and activity should be strictly controlled and limited. He should not receive any liquor unless he has a copy of the purchase order, which is the only authorization to receive. If there is any discrepancy between the purchase order and the invoice, he is not allowed to accept delivery unless he obtains approval from the purchasing agent or the manager. If a bottle has been broken, the unit value is subtracted from the invoice which is then signed by both the delivery man and the storeroom man.

2. The storeroom man has the *only* key for the storeroom. Thus, he is completely responsible for any inventory shortages.

3. The responsibility and authority to store and to issue have been separated and fixed. The storeroom man cannot remove liquor from the storeroom without a properly signed requisition from the bartender, because only an *authorized* withdrawal can reduce the perpetual liquor inventory record held by the office. If an unauthorized withdrawal from stores occurs, a discrepancy will be revealed between the figures in the physical inventory in the storeroom and the perpetual inventory held by the office. The storeroom man cannot permanently misstate additions or withdrawals of liquor, because the original purchase order and bar requisition are held by the office.

4. The bartender cannot requisition indiscriminately. His request for issues is governed by his par stock and, subsequently, by his empties. The number, size, and brand of empty bottles is checked by the liquor cost controller.

5. The bartender cannot alter his requisition later and state that he received less, because the original requisition is held by the office and a copy is retained by the liquor cost controller.

Part 3—Control of Liquor Sales

IMPORTANCE OF LIQUOR SALES CONTROL

MANY COMPETENT OPERATORS have installed a system that provides adequate control of the purchasing, receiving, storing, and issuing of liquor. However, the control of sales has generally been inadequate. The need for effective control of liquor sales is most important; it is the final phase that translates physical goods into gross income. It is also the phase in which avarice, carelessness, and theft are the most prevalent!

The sale of liquor differs in two important respects from the other functions. First, the physical handling of money is involved. Secondly, where liquor sales are large, responsibility is difficult to fix on any one of the many bartenders.

THE BARTENDER AND LIQUOR SALES CONTROL

The human element involved in liquor sales presents a very difficult problem of control. A bartender is constantly faced with the pressure to be a "good fellow" in order to increase his tips and with the temptation to pocket a little of the seemingly endless flow of money between customer and cash register. The results of being a "good fellow" or not resisting temptation are usually "drinks on the house," a larger portion of liquor for the same price, or theft of cash or liquor, with a subsequent proportionate increase of cost.

Some bartenders' ingenuity for devising new methods of theft is imaginative and extensive. It may range from short-changing the customer, or ringing up the sale of two drinks instead of three, to bringing in and selling his own liquor over the bar. Management has countered with preventives ranging from the hiring of business services to check on their bartenders, to distinctive bottle marks, or a surprise reading of register tapes.

In any case, the major argument against this type of cost control is the system's concentration of control on the human element. First, it is singularly difficult to observe the activities of several bartenders every minute and hour during the day. Secondly, overly close supervision lowers the morale and, in many cases, promotes theft or carelessness. The personal conflict between the observer and the observed creates a loser's contest. Bartenders who resent constant observation have been known to empty an entire bottle of liquor down the drain as they smiled at the manager or owner who is standing across the room.

Finally, the concept of controlling the human element is fallacious because it detracts from considering the single inanimate item that *can* be controlled—the liquor itself!

A proper approach is to create a system of liquor cost control that is practical in time and cost and that is efficient and based on administrative policy—not personal supervision.

OUTLINE OF LIQUOR SALES CONTROL

The correct method is to base the system on the analysis of sales and consumption of liquor. In outline form, the approach to cost control of liquor sales is as follows:

1. Standardize all mixed drinks and instruct bartenders to mix according to stated proportions.

2. Determine how much liquor will be served in straight drinks for a given price and then see that the instructions are followed.

3. Install a checking system in which all checks are serially numbered and determine the office procedure necessary to account for each.

4. Determine and prepare a system of recorded information that will gather, evaluate, and interpret the data so management can account for the differences between the liquor sales and consumption.

STANDARDIZATION OF LIQUOR

There are two reasons for standardizing mixed drinks and regulating the amount of liquor sold as a straight drink. First, if the quantity of each drink sold is standardized, management can very easily discover how much liquor was consumed on any day's sales by analyzing the beverage sales checks. Secondly, because the amount of each ingredient in the mixed drink has been regulated, the patron is able to obtain the identical taste and flavor of his favorite drink in any bar or section of the bar in the operation. For example, he will be able to depend on the fact that a Martini ordered in one section of the bar on one day will taste the same as the Martini ordered in another section the next day.

Therefore, it follows that the taste of the mixed drink will vary only according to the standards set up by management policy, not because of the personal idiosyncracies of the bartenders. The duty of the head bartender, in conjunction with the manager, is to set a high standard for drinks so that the patron will be content with the quality and the bar will obtain the amount of revenue necessary to keep its cost at a desired level.

EFFECTIVE PRICING OF LIQUOR

The prices of various brands of liquor are determined after considering cost, competition, and promotional factors. In terms of liquor cost alone, the price of each drink is very simply the cost of the bottle, divided by the number of drinks the bottle contains, and multiplied by the factor that will give the operator the desired liquor cost percentage.

The realistic operator might reduce the number of drinks available in each bottle by 1 or 2 percent to allow for the small amount of liquor lost through carelessness, evaporation, and spillage.

In the following two illustrations, Example 1 and Example 2, let us assume that the operator desires a 30 percent liquor cost. The factor that will give him this liquor cost percentage is 3.33 (or 100 divided by 30).

EXAMPLE 1

1. Cost of quart bottle	$5.65
2. Number of one oz. drinks mathematically available in qt.	32.
3. Two percent reduction due to spillage, etc.	.64
4. Number of one oz. drinks actually available 32.-.64 or	31.4
5. Cost per drink $5.65/31.4 or	.18
6. Estimated selling price 3.33 (.18) =	.60

EXAMPLE 2
Golden Martini

Proportion: 1-1/2 oz. yellow gin, 1 oz. vermouth.

1. Cost of qt. bottle gin	$5.65
2. Cost of qt. bottle dry vermouth	$1.10
3. Number of 1-1/2 oz. drinks mathematically available in qt. gin	21.3
4. Two percent reduction due to spillage, etc.	.40
5. Number of 1-1/2 oz. drinks actually available	20.9
6. Cost of gin $5.65/20.9 or	.27
7. Number of 1 oz. drinks available in qt. vermouth	32.
8. Two percent reduction due to spillage etc.	31.4
9. Cost of vermouth serving $1.88/31.4 or	.06
10. Total cost Golden Martini, step 6 plus step 9 or 27 cents plus 6 cents or	.33
11. Estimated selling price 3.33 (.33) or	$1.10

EFFECTS OF COMPETITION OR PROMOTION ON SELLING PRICE

In both illustrations the term "estimated selling price" has been used because the factors of competition, promotion, and price manipulation have not been considered. In terms of competition, if a nearby bar sells a similar straight drink for 70 cents and a Golden Martini for $1.00, the prices can be adjusted, depending on the percentage of sales of each drink, to 75 cents and $1.00 respectively without disturbing the desired liquor cost percentage.

On the other hand, when the promotional factor is considered, this type of adjustment may not be necessary. If the primary purpose of the promotion is to enlarge the volume of business, the problem of pricing resolves itself by retaining the 60 cent drink, and either purchasing a lower cost gin in order to meet the price level of the competitor or deciding to sell the cocktail for $1.00 regardless of liquor percentage. In either case, the operator has the factual material necessary to arrive at a satisfactory, intelligent price decision.

The importance of increased sales volume and price manipulation has been discussed thoroughly in the preceding sections. The successful manager uses pricing as another basic tool to accomplish specific objectives regarding his ultimate goal, which is to increase profit. He is fully aware that he cannot bank a percentage—only dollars— and he concentrates on

the single objective of manipulating price and other factors so
that sales volume and gross profit are increased. Some examples: a Playboy Club combines atmosphere and a high average check and may sell a 1-1/2 oz. drink for $2.00. A bar de-
cides to sell a bottle of domestic beer for 30 cents and a bottle
of imported beer for 50 cents to increase the average check.
Another bar provides peanuts, pretzels, and cheddar cheese
spread to increase its sales. A motel places cards in the motel
rooms informing its guests that in the dining room during the
happy hour between 5 and 6 p.m., any drink may be purchased for 65 cents. The purpose, of course, is to increase not
only liquor sales in the dining room but also food sales. The
manager first determines his objective and then utilizes every
skill or tool, including pricing, to achieve his goal.

IMPORTANCE OF PRICE UNIFORMITY

The second important consideration of effective pricing is
uniformity. Aside from the cost structure, a uniform predetermined level of prices must be in force along the length of
the entire bar. The prices of the popular highballs, cocktails,
and straight drinks are generally conspicuously posted on the
beverage list.

However, there are many drinks that are requested which,
for expediency or because of limited space, are omitted from
the beverage list. A patron may ask for a Rob Roy made with
Johnny Walker Red Label, a Bourbon Manhattan made with
Old Grand Dad, a Martini "extra, extra dry," one of a thous-
and concoctions contained in bar or drink-mixing guides, or
perhaps even an invention of his own.

A competent operator determines these prices by using his
knowledge of past experience, his immediate environment, and
his awareness of the costs involved. He knows his patrons and
their requests in the past, the average cost of the brands involved in drinks mixed with a designated brand, and the detailed costs of the less popular drinks. After these prices are
determined, he posts them behind each bar station.

In any case, bartenders should not be given the authority to
quote their own prices: first, because their prices may not be
correct in terms of cost; secondly, because the price set arbitrarily by one bartender will differ from the price determined
by another; thirdly, because the bartender may forget the

charge he set previously and ask a different price from the same patron. Thus, the patron is faced with a bewildering array of prices depending on the section of the bar in which he is being served and the mood of the bartender.

GLASSWARE AND ITS EFFECT ON CONTROL

Another important factor in liquor cost control is the size of glassware. The question of size must be carefully determined to fit the needs of the operation and to make it difficult for the bartender to give the patron more than he has paid for.

For example, if the straight drink has been standardized at 1 oz., the size of the whiskey glass should not be much more. When the whiskey glass is 1-1/2 oz., a bartender with a "heavy hand" will pour about one-quarter of an ounce more for each sale, increasing liquor cost by 25 percent. On the other hand, if the whiskey glass is exactly 1 oz., the bartender may overfill the glass to show his customer that he is trying to please him or the patron may spill the brimming glass as he attempts to place it to his lips. In either case, the liquor given away, spilled on the bar or on the customer, is money and goodwill lost. The proper sized glass in this instance would seem to be a 1-1/4-oz. glass with a 7/8-oz. line. The bartender should be instructed to always pour slightly above the line, and he will be pleased to do so because he can show his customer that he is going "over the line" for him (and for a good tip). The patron is happy about the "extra" service and the fact that he can drink comfortably without spilling. And the owner is happy to obtain an equitable price for the liquor sold!

Similarly, the size of the glassware for the mixed drinks is determined according to the standards that have been set. To illustrate, the size of a cocktail glass containing a 2-1/2-oz. Manhattan can be determined by volume of liquid and its appearance in the glass. Generally, the cocktail glass has a wide brim and narrow bottom. Because of the wide brim, a minimum of 1 oz. allowance must be made to improve the sales appeal of the cocktail and to prevent spillage. Therefore, a 3-1/2-oz. glass or a 4-oz. glass with a 2-1/2-oz. line would fit the desired specification.

Control of liquor in this case is also obtained by the standard formula. For example, the bartender may be instructed to mix a Manhattan in the ratio of 1-1/2 oz. of bar rye to 1 oz. of sweet vermouth. The bartender will pour the bar rye into the jigger and pour 1 oz. of sweet vermouth into the pony, empty this into the mixing glass, stir the mixture, and pour the Manhattan into a chilled cocktail glass. The finished cocktail will flow over the 2-1/2 oz. line because during the stirring, the liquid content was increased by the melting ice. Once again, the bartender, the patron, and the standards of the operation will be satisfied.

USE OF LIQUOR CHECKS

The next step in the control of liquor sales is the installation of a checking system that will serve as a record of liquor sales and also as a record of the number and types of total liquor sold.

Generally, the checks are serially numbered and, through the use of identifying letters, numbers, or colors cannot be used for any bar station other than that for which the checks were issued. The numbered checks are issued to the bartenders and to the cocktail lounge waitresses or waiters only against their signature. Before the bar opens for business, the required number of checks is prepared for each person and then issued in numerical order. At the end of his work period, each employee returns the unused checks, and the closing number of each checkbook is recorded. Later the cashier or office personnel place the used bar checks in numerical order for each bar or station and check for missing checks, mistakes in pricing, and other inaccuracies. The sum of the prices on the checks should equal the total of liquor sales rung on the register.

Very few checking systems are satisfactory in presenting to management a recorded, complete sales breakdown of all liquor sold for any particular day; yet, the sales analysis of the total liquor sold is the most reliable method of controlling costs.

To illustrate on a small scale, if an owner's beginning inventory is 12 qt. of rye and his ending inventory is 9 qt., and if there is no record of amount and type of liquor sold, the only single valid statement he can make is that three bottles of rye were consumed. Without the necessary data to analyze his rye sales, he does not know how much of this consumption was registered as sales, given away, or lost in a cash transaction.

The manager or head bartender should instruct the bartenders that before a patron is served, a check must be made out with the patron's order written in indelible pencil or pen. There are several good reasons for this procedure. During the rush period, even an honest bartender can forget how many drinks he served any one party, or the fact that a patron may have shifted from an 80 cent to a $1.00 drink. Also, since the bartender must write the patron's order and its price with indelible pencil, he cannot alter the check later to take cash from the register, to charge the patron less for a greater tip, or to charge more and pocket the difference. Furthermore, the manager can check his control of sales more easily by noting whether a check is or is not visible in front of each customer, whether a bartender is writing down his orders, and whether there are any discrepancies between the value of the liquor that the customer has been served and the amount rung on the register. Finally, the check provides for management a record of liquor sold and for the customer a record of price of the drinks.

To forestall the bartender's objection that he does not have time to write the complete order when his station is busy, the manager or liquor cost controller should devise an easily learned, abbreviated form to record the desired information.

Since most drink control systems deal only with types of liquor and not with brand names, a simple code should be determined for these types. The abbreviations should be easily associated with the type of liquor involved. For example, rye, scotch, gin, bourbon, Manhattan, and Martini can be written R, Sc, Gin, Bour, Man and Mt, respectively. A bartender hearing an order for Seagram's Seven Crown, Canadian Club, Old Forrester, or Bourbon Manhattan would write, for example: R. 50¢, R. 65¢, Bour. 70¢, B. Man. 75¢.

After the check has been paid, but not before the patron leaves, it is rung on the register and placed in a secured locked box. In the morning, a member of the office personnel removes the checks from the bar and looks through them for agreement with total liquor sales on the register tape, for incorrect pricing, and for missing checks.

CASH CONTROLS

Although professional management is regarded as completely honest, it is still practical from the owner's point of view to remove all temptation. If the night manager or the cashier has the authority to count the cash at night and to make a final reading on the register tape, he is unnecessarily exposed to the temptation to pocket any overages. It is more prudent to separate these two activities. Generally, it is wiser to have the night manager or the cashier count the cash, make a record of the amount, and deposit the cashier's envelope in the safe. The office personnel should have the register keys to make a reading in the morning and compare register sales with amount of cash turned in by the night manager.

The second element of cash control is concerned with the sale of liquor and the receiving of money by the waiters or waitresses. Where this is done, because of a problem with walk-outs or for any other reason, effective control can be established by giving each waiter or waitress a house bank which is properly receipted at the beginning of his or her work period.

The service personnel are instructed to obtain all their liquor at the service bar. The guide rail, a few feet from the bar, aids them in obtaining their orders and leads them to the cashier-checker who compares the items on the tray with the liquor recorded on the check. The checker obtains the money and stamps the prices received for each item—the cost to the patron—by inserting the check in the register and recording each sale.

Each person serving liquor is given an indelible pencil to write out the order and to total the printed sales. After the patron pays, the beverage checks are returned to the checker-cashier who reviews the additions and the tax charge, then drops the completed checks in a locked box.

SUMMARY OF CONTROLS AT THE BAR

In summary, these are the important things to remember about bar controls.

The bartender's authority to requisition liquor should be limited. He can initiate a requisition by writing the details and signing the numbered, triplicate beverage requisition form. Moreover, the amount and type of liquor he requisitions is limited by the par stock and the empty bottle control. The storeroom man checks the requisition, makes a record of the authorized withdrawals on the bin cards (his perpetual inventory), signs the beverage requisition form, and issues the liquor. The bartender indicates by signature that he received the liquor and keeps one copy of the completed form, forwarding the original to the office so that the bookkeeper can record the issues on the stock ledger—the perpetual liquor inventory in the office.

At this point the control on bottled liquor is almost complete. The maximum inventory level established for liquor purchases, liquor in the storeroom and in the bar, reduces the possibility of theft because quantities are limited; and it increases inventory turnover which, in turn, increases profit on a given investment.

The paper forms and policy decisions actually have four different employees providing checks on one another. Control of purchasing and paying has been discussed. The beverage requisition, the stock ledger, and the various limitations of action are now superimposed on the control system.

Accordingly, there is no way for the accountant or the bartender to remove a bottle of liquor without being discovered, because a physical inventory is taken by another employee in a different department. The bartender cannot say he received only 2 bottles instead of 3 or reduce the number of bottles on the bar requisition, because the other 2 completed copies have been distributed to the storeroom man and the accountant.

The storeroom man would have to be fairly naive to issue 3 bottles and join forces with the bartender and write 2 on the beverage requisition, because the stock ledger in the office would be reduced by only 2 bottles. Discovery is instant when a physical inventory of the storeroom is compared with the perpetual inventory in the office.

Regarding the control of drink sales and cash, all of the following subcontrols should be noted. Most of them can be implemented in any bar.

1. *Numbered beverage requisition forms and perpetual inventory forms in the storeroom and the office should be employed. These forms create a 3-way check on bartender, storeroom man, and accountant.*

2. *Dressing rooms should be apart from the cocktail lounge, and close fitting uniforms issued to prevent liquor being transported to or away from the bar. An on-duty bartender who is given a package by a customer, or picks up a package left by a customer, is suspect.*

3. *Place a distinctive stamp on all bottles to discourage bartenders from bringing in their own liquor.*

4. *Empty bottle control: no liquor should be issued without an empty bottle given.*

5. *All mixed drinks should be made according to a standard drink recipe using standardized ingredients.*

6. *All drinks should be measured using appropriate jiggers, ponys, or glassware.*

7. *All liquor glassware is to be standardized.*

8. *No bartender should be allowed to determine the price of a drink. Price determination is a management decision.*

9. *All liquor sold must be entered indelibly on a numbered, tinted check. At the bar, the check should be placed with the blank side facing the customer at all times.*

10. *No checks should be visible near the cash register. Bartenders should not be permitted to give the customer change without recording the register sale. After a sale has been recorded, the bartender should be instructed to place completed checks in locked box near register. No completed check should be available to the bartender.*

11. *All checks should be put in numerical sequence and inspected for missing checks, improper prices, etc.*

12. *Voided checks should require the signature and approval of an employee other than the bartender.*

13. *Place lights over the register so that amount rung up is clearly visible.*

14. *Consider the use of spotters or outside agency personnel to discourage theft and to improve service and customer relations.*

15. *The read key to the register should not be available to any bartender.*

16. *Make random, surprise register readings. Whenever a customer is short-changed or payment has been received for 4 drinks and only 3 have been rung on the register, there is an increase in cash. No bartender is naive enough to believe that he can take money out of the register 20 times without being observed by someone. Therefore, he has 2 options: as a self-appointed, unofficial partner he can remove the $20 bill either soon after he begins his shift, or he can remove the money toward the end of his work day. In either case, a surprise cash register reading and a count of the cash will reveal the shortage or the overage.*

17. *The register tape and the subsequent register reading must agree with the cash received and the total of the sales checks.*

18. *No bartender should be permitted to give drinks on the house. If he wishes to do this, he should be advised to open*

up his own bar somewhere else and give away his own liquor.

19. Neither the owner nor the manager should be allowed to have a free drink or to give a drink to a customer without signing a check so a record exists. They should not be allowed in the storeroom without the storeroom man being present to make a record of the withdrawal.

Part 4 — Formal Control Systems

REASONS FOR MORE COMPLEX SYSTEMS

ALL OF THE controls on employees and on liquor that are covered in the following pages may be installed in any operation serving liquor. Not only are these controls relatively inexpensive, but also they will establish considerable security and order along the base floor of the profit pyramid. In many instances, these controls alone may be sufficient.

However, large-volume bar operations may want to have more precise controls which can provide additional detailed information regarding sales, sales trends, and pricing policies so that more effective management decisions can be made.

There are two primary methods of formally controlling liquor: (1) a daily inventory and (2) a two- or four-week inventory based on a specified financial period.

THE FIRST FORMAL CONTROL SYSTEM

The first method of formal control is determined by the relationship between the amount of money that should be in the register and the quantity of liquor consumed. Liquor consumption can be broken down into two categories: mixed and straight drinks by the glass and bottle sales. A daily bar control form provides the basic information regarding details of liquor consumption, and a daily sales distribution sheet provides the sales data.

A very simple example can illustrate the basic premise of this type of formal control. A bar called Ye Olde Gin Mill serves only Carstairs gin that sells for 70 cents an oz.

A daily physical inventory is taken and this
reveals | 10 qt.
The total issued from the storeroom is | 8 qt.

The total liquor available is   18 qt.
An ending inventory is taken revealing
   only 8 qt. remaining   -8 qt.
Total liquor consumed   10 qt.

Since all drinks are 1 oz. and are sold for 75 cents and there are 32 oz. to a qt., there should be 75 cents x 320 or $240 in the cash register. The money in the cash register is counted. If there is $240 in the cash register, there are no problems. If there is $250 in the cash register, some customer or customers were shortchanged $10. On the other hand, if the register shows only $232.50, there is a $7.50 shortage, and the sales value of 10 gin drinks is missing.

SOME PROBLEMS OF THE FIRST SYSTEM

In this very simple illustration, both an inventory and a sales analysis must be made *every day*. If the daily inventory and the daily sales analysis are not made, the resulting data is simply an estimate and cannot be considered totally accurate.

There are other problems with this system that must be resolved. What if all drinks were not sold for 75 cents and some drinks contained more than 1 oz. of liquor? For example, Ye Olde Gin Mill expands its beverage list so bar customers may have a variety of selections: a Martini containing 2 oz. of gin is $1.10, an Orange Blossom with 1-1/2 oz. sells for 90 cents, a Tom Collins containing 1 oz. is 80 cents, and a Gin on the Rocks measuring 1 oz. is 60 cents. In the dining room each drink is increased by 10 cents, and there is a $12.80 charge for full bottles.

The determination of how much money should be in the cash register is now complicated considerably. The manager cannot take the information from the sales checks or the sales analysis sheet because the checks have already been rung up on the register.

If the transactions were performed accurately, the sum of the waiters' checks would be equal to the amount of money in the register. The total will tell management the dollar value of the liquor recorded, but *not the amount consumed*.

Since quantities and prices vary, the only method of determining the value of consumption is to assign a basic sales value to the liquor consumed and assign sales differentials to each drink that has a variance in price or in quantity. To eliminate errors and to simplify the mathematics, the basic sales value is determined according to the sales value of the most popular drink sold. A sales history will provide the manager with this information for each brand of liquor that is sold. At Ye Olde Gin Mill, the most popular way to sell gin is as the 1 oz. drink of Gin on the Rocks for 75 cents. Therefore, 75 cents per oz. is the basic sales value of all the gin consumed. The Bar Control Form indicates that 10 qt., or 320 oz., were consumed. The basic sales is 320 x 75 cents or $240 basic sales value for all the gin consumed.

The sales differentials are determined by noting the difference between the 75 cents basic sales value per oz. and the selling price of each drink. The determination is made using the following method.

Subtracting a 10 cent value for the vermouth, the two oz. Martini selling for $1.10 has a sales value of 50 cents an oz. The price difference for the Martini is -5 cents an oz. or -50 cents a drink

An Orange Blossom contains 1-1/2 oz. of gin valued at 90 cents. Therefore, the sales value per oz. is 60 cents and the difference for the Orange Blossom is -15 cents per oz. or -22.5 cents per drink

A Tom Collins contains 1 oz. and sells for 80 cents. Therefore, the sales value per oz. is 80 cents and the price difference for a Tom Collins is +5 cents

For every drink sold in the private dining room there is a 10 cent service charge. The price difference for each drink is +10 cents

Each bottle contains 32 oz. and sells for $12.80 or 40 cents an oz. The price difference per oz. is -35 cents or per bottle is $11.25

Gin on the rocks contains 1 oz. and is sold for 75 cents, so this is not considered at all. There is no difference between the sales price per oz. of Gin on the Rocks or the basic sales value of all liquor consumed.

The sales analysis sheet provides management with the following details of liquor sales. The information comes from the waiters' checks. The actual drink sales columns have been omitted.

AT THE BAR

	Unit Differential	Total Basic Value
128 Gin on the Rocks 25 Martinis 20 Orange Blossoms 16 Tom Collins		

PRIVATE DINING ROOM

	Unit Differential	Total Basic Value
33 Gin on the Rocks 10 Martinis 6 Orange Blossoms 2 Tom Collins 1 bottle gin		

The controller adds the price differentials that have been predetermined to the respective drink or bottle sales. The completed form, minus the actual sales column, is shown in the following charts.

AT THE BAR

	Unit Differential	Total Basic Value
128 Gin on the Rocks	0	0
25 Martinis	–.50	–12.50
20 Orange Blossoms	–.225	–4.50
16 Tom Collins	+.05	+.80
Net sales value difference –$16.10		

PRIVATE DINING ROOM

	Unit Differential	Total Basic Value
33 Gin on the Rocks	0	0
10 Martinis	–.50	–5.00
6 Orange Blossoms	–.225	–1.35
2 Tom Collins	+.05	+.10
1 bottle gin	–11.25	–.11.25
Net sales value difference –$17.50		

The basic sales value of all liquor consumed   = $240.00
The net sales value difference is (-$16.10) +
  (-$17.50)=   -33.60

               Gross basic sales value   = $206.40
Fifty drinks sold in dining room at +10 cents
  service differential   =   +5.00

Amount of money that should be in the bar
  register   = $211.40

If this method is regarded as too complicated, then the manager of a bar had better stay far away from this particular system. The difficulties have just begun.

Here is another aspect to think about. Ye Olde Gin Mill sells only one brand of gin. So, price differentials are calculated for the various ways Carstairs gin is sold. If several brands of gin are sold at varying prices and quantities, then price, bottle, and service differentials will have to be determined for each difference in price from the basic sale value. Moreover, bars and cocktail lounges in general do not sell just a few brands of gin. Their beverage list is complete with a variety of gin, scotch, bourbon, rye, vodka, rum, cordials, liqueurs, brandies, and domestic and imported wines and beer. Consequently, if only 5 different brands in each liquor group are sold at 4 different price variances from the basic sales value, the manager would have to use 65 basic sales values and 260 price differentials every day to determine the amount of money in the cash register.

However, with all the other features of the system omitted, it is not fair to arbitrarily decide that the sales system is too time-consuming and ineffective. It is true that for the data to be accurate and meaningful the system requires a great deal of time. Nevertheless, if the volume of sales is large enough to afford a liquor cost controller, or a combination food and liquor cost controller, this approach has considerable merit and effectively aids in the control of cash and costs for drinks and mixed drinks, bottle sales, dry liquor group, and for the entire operation.

THE SECOND FORMAL SYSTEM

The second formal control system does not require daily inventories, basic sales values, or price differentials. The controls can determine shortages or overages by the drink, the bottle, the liquor group, and for the entire operation. This system can pinpoint the same details of sales and cost trends or provide detailed information for effective management decisions.

Though this system is also based on consumption of liquor, the simplifying difference is that controls are established through a comparison of *recorded* sales, thus eliminating all basic sales values determinations and price, bottle, and service differentials. And, daily inventories are eliminated! Only a beginning and ending inventory are required during the entire financial period—generally, a two- or four-week period depending on the concern of the owner. Finally, since liquor is completely controlled up to the time that it is issued to the bar, only the liquor at the bar is inventoried.

A simple example can illustrate the basic concept. The manager determines that 70 qt. of rye were consumed, at a cost of $350. Sales of rye during this period were $1,155. 70 quarts are equivalent to 2,240 1-oz. drinks. The summary for the period indicates that only 2,233 drinks were sold and recorded in the register. Consequently, in the rye liquor group, a shortage of seven 1-oz. drinks occurred. Also, the cost of rye sales is 30 percent.

Because this system eliminates the daily inventory problem and other time-consuming factors; because it provides the owner or manager with considerable information that he would not otherwise have to control the cost and sales of liquor at the bar; and because it is very inexpensive and easy to understand and use, the quantity liquor control system is explained in detail on the following pages. The procedures that follow can very easily be completed in less than one-and-a-half-hours a day even if daily liquor sales are over $1,200. After working with the forms several times, the paper work is rapid and easy. It is advisable to obtain an overview of the system by first studying the two master monthly summaries and their interpretation on pages 158 through 172; then returning to the material that follows this paragraph.

DAILY BEVERAGE ALLOCATION SHEETS

The purpose of the Daily Beverage Allocation Sheet is to provide the beverage cost controller with a series of printed forms so that he may record the following information: the total number of each individual type of liquor sold daily, the revenue obtained from each type, the total number of sales of all liquor sold, and the allocation of each drink to the type of liquor involved, with its proportionate cost. These sheets are the basis of the drink control sales and cost analysis.

Depending on the diversification and volume of liquor business, the Daily Beverage Allocation Sheets (Figure 4) are usually 4 or 5 in number and are designed to facilitate a comprehensive, classified analysis of types and total liquor sold.

The beverage cost controller begins his analysis of consumption by going through each individual beverage check. Every item on the check is recorded by placing a tally mark in the appropriate space on the Daily Beverage Allocation Sheet. After all the items are recorded according to type of liquor involved and price of sale, the tally marks are totaled for each item and recorded on the sheet. These totals are subsequently multiplied by their selling price to obtain the sales value of each type of liquor sold. In several operations where this system has been installed, the use of a multi-counter with the Daily Beverage Allocation Sheets can speed up the work considerably.

The number of all drinks sold within a specific liquor category subsequently forms the basis of consumption control for that liquor. Similarly, the total sales value of any single group is the basis for the sales analysis of that group.

PROPER SALES ALLOCATION OF MIXED DRINKS

The final phase of the analysis in the Daily Beverage Allocation Sheets is the equitable distribution of sales among the types of liquor involved. There is no problem of allocation in the case of straight drinks, for the total sales value can be applied against one type of liquor. However, mixed drinks or cocktails in which at least two types of liquor are needed for preparation do constitute a problem in proper allocation.

Therefore, management must decide on one of two methods for allocating the beverage sales. The first method of allocation is based on the relative cost of the liquors involved. Thus, in any given mixed drink the relationship between the required quantity of each liquor and its relative cost is determined. The sales value is allocated according to this determination.

For example, assume a Manhattan Cocktail has been standardized at 2-1/2 oz. That is, 1 oz. of rye and 1-1/2 oz. of sweet vermouth are needed for each drink. The price of the Manhattan is $1.00.

FIGURE 4

Location Capital Cocktail Lounge   Station   1

DAILY BEVERAGE ALLOCATION SHEET

Date   June 1, 19   Day Wednesday

	No. of Drinks Sold	Total Sales		
Rye			Rye	Vermouth
50¢				
50¢	83	$41.50		
55¢	40	22.00		
55¢				
60¢	32	19.20		
65¢	30	13.00		
75¢				
80¢	7	5.60		
85¢				
Sub Total	192	$107.80	$107.80	
Manhattans				
65¢				
65¢	123	$79.95		
75¢	15	11.25		
85¢	10	8.50		
90¢				
Sub Total	148	$99.70	$ 72.78	$26.92
Rye Bottles				
$8.50	6-5's	$51.00		
9.00	4-5's	36.00		
10.00				
Sub Total	10-5's	$87.00	$ 87.00	
Vermouth				
30¢	7	$ 2.10		
45¢	2	.90		
Sub Total	9	$ 3.00		$ 3.00

(Cont.)

FIGURE 4 (Cont.)

Location_Capital Cocktail Lounge   Station____1____

DAILY BEVERAGE ALLOCATION SHEET

Date_June 1, 19__   Day_Wednesday___

	No. of Drinks Sold	Total Sales		
Gin 50¢			Gin	Vermouth
50¢	30	$15.00		
50¢	10	5.50		
60¢				
60¢	54	32.40		
65¢	3	1.95		
70¢	2	1.40		
Sub Total	99	$56.25	$56.25	
Martinis 60¢				
60¢	97	$58.20		
70¢	12	8.40		
75¢	4	3.00		
80¢	2	1.60		
Sub Total	115	$71.20	$51.98	$19.22
Scotch Manhattans			Scotch	
75¢	32	$24.00		
85¢	10	8.50		
Sub Total	42	$32.50	$26.00	$ 6.50
Bourbon Manhattans			Bourbon	
70¢	14	$ 9.80		
75¢	2	1.50		
80¢	1	.80		
Sub Total	17	$12.10	$ 9.05	$ 3.05

Location Capital Cocktail Lounge   Station   1

DAILY BEVERAGE ALLOCATION SHEET

Date   June 1, 19   Day Wednesday

	No. of Drinks Sold	Total Sales	
Scotch 60¢			Scotch
60¢	75	$45.00	
65¢	20	13.00	
70¢	13	9.10	
75¢	15	11.25	
80¢	6	4.80	
85¢	4	3.40	
Sub Total	133	$86.55	$86.55
Scotch, bottles			
$11.00	4	$44.00	
12.50	4	50.00	
Sub Total	8	$94.00	$94.00
Sub Total			$180.55
Bourbon			Bourbon
60¢	14	$ 8.40	
65¢	7	4.55	
75¢	9	6.75	
80¢	3	2.40	
Sub Total	33	$22.10	$22.10
Bourbon, bottles			
$10.00			
11.50			
12.50			
Sub Total			
Cordials			Cordials
60¢	27	$16.20	
65¢	12	7.80	
70¢			
75¢	9	6.75	
80¢	2	1.60	
Sub Total	50	$32.35	$32.35

(Cont.)

FIGURE 4 (Cont.)

Location Capital Cocktail Lounge .   Station 1

DAILY BEVERAGE ALLOCATION SHEET

Date   June 1, 19   Day Wednesday

	No. of Drinks Sold	Total Sales	Cordials	Gin
Cordials (mixed)				
75¢ Alexander	6	$ 4.50	$ 1.50	$3.00
80¢ Alaska Cocktail	3	2.40	.80	1.60
75¢ Singapore Sling	3	2.25	1.12	1.13
Sub Total	12		$ 3.42	$5.73
Cordials (mixed)				Brandy
75¢ Side Car	7	$ 5.25	$ 2.72	$2.73
75¢ Stinger	4	3.00	1.00	2.00
75¢ Brandy Alexander	5	3.75	1.25	2.50
80¢ Angel's Kiss	2	1.60	1.05	.55
Sub Total	18		$ 6.02	$7.78
Draught Beer 15			Beer	
15¢	136	$20.40		
20¢	70	14.00		
Sub Total	206	$34.40	$34.40	
Bottle Beer 40				
40¢	84	$ 33.60		
60¢	12	7.20		
85¢	2	1.70		
Sub Total	98	$ 42.50	$42.50	
Coke, Sodas, etc. 20			Sodas	
20¢	42	8.40	$ 8.40	
Misc.,Orangeades, etc.,35			Misc.	
35¢	2	.70	.70	

Location Capital Cocktail Lounge Station 1

DAILY BEVERAGE ALLOCATION SHEET

Date June 1, 19 Day Wednesday

	No. of Drinks Sold	Total Sales	Brandy
Brandy 50			
50¢	27	$13.50	
60¢	5	3.00	
70¢	7	4.90	
85¢	7	5.95	
Sub Total	46	$27.35	$27.35
Rum 60			Rum
60¢	43	$25.80	
65¢			
65¢	62	40.30	
70¢	6	4.20	
75¢	3	2.25	
Sub Total	114	$72.55	$72.55
Wine 35			Wine
35¢	9	$ 3.15	
40¢	12	4.80	
50¢	7	3.50	
75¢			
90¢			
$1.00	2	2.00	
Sub Total	30	$13.45	$13.45
Wine, bottles 2.50			
$4.00	4	$16.00	$16.00
8.00			
Sub Total			$29.45

(Cont.)

Cost of one qt. bar rye	$ 4.40
Cost of 1-1/2 qt. sweet vermouth	1.60
Total cost of Manhattans	$ 6.00
Proportionate cost of rye $4.40/6.00 = 11/15 =	73%
Proportionate cost of sweet vermouth	
$1.60/6.00 = 4/15 =	27%
Total sales of Manhattans for day	$66.95
Allocation of sales to rye .73 ($66.95) =	48.87
Allocation of sales to sweet vermouth	
.27 ($66.95) =	18.08

The second method of allocating beverage sales is based on the sales price of each drink ingredient as if it were sold singly. The allocation of total sales is determined by the relationship of these individual sales prices among the various drink ingredients to the total sales.

The Manhattan mentioned earlier may serve to make this method of allocation clearer.

The liquor ingredients of a Manhattan are standardized at 1 oz. of rye and 1-1/2 oz. of sweet vermouth.

The sales value of 1 oz. bar rye	$ .50
Sales value of 1-1/2 oz. vermouth	.30
Total sales value	$ .80
Proportionate sales value of rye $.50/.80 = 5/8 =	63%
Proportionate sales value of sweet vermouth	
$.30/.80 = 3/8 =	37%
Total sales of Manhattans for day	$66.95
Allocation of sales to rye .63 ($66.95) =	42.18
Allocation of sales to sweet vermouth	
.37 ($66.95) =	24.77

RATIONALE FOR SALES ALLOCATION

To summarize: The first method states that, where proper pricing is in effect, the sales value of any mixed drink accrues to a single ingredient in proportion to the cost of that ingredient, and that this initial cost is the proper measure of the mixed drink's relative sales allocation. The second method is based on the premise that when two or more ingredients are mixed, the resulting drink should be regarded as completely different in its contribution to sales volume.

The proponents of the second method argue that it is not realistic to allocate sales value to drink ingredients in proportion to their cost. Their reasoning is that in several instances sales volume would not materialize unless, or until, the ingredients are mixed. For example, relatively few drinks of straight gin or dry vermouth can be sold to patrons. However, when these two ingredients are combined in a Martini, the sale of gin and vermouth is considerably increased.

The owner-manager should decide on one method or the other, or perhaps a combination of both, according to the information he wants reflected in the sales analysis. The most important point to consider is that whichever method of allocating sales is finally determined, that method must be followed consistently in all future allocations. In the Daily Beverage Allocation Sheets illustrated in Figure 4, the allocation of sales has been made on the basis of costs.

THE SUMMARY DAILY BEVERAGE ALLOCATION SALES SHEET

The Daily Beverage Allocation Sheets are summarized in the Summary Daily Allocation Beverage Sales (Figure 5). The beverage cost controller must correctly fill in the name of the cocktail lounge, the bar station under control, the date, and the day on which the liquor sales occurred. Then, he must transfer the total number of each type of liquor sold and its allocated sales from the Daily Beverage Allocation Sheets to the Summary Sheet as illustrated on pages 150-152.

The first column, entitled No. of Drinks Sold, is the basis of the consumption control for the day, and the remaining columns record the data for the sales analysis. When this summary is completed, the beverage cost controller must reconcile the grand total of all liquor sold with the sales total shown by the combined register tapes in the beverage department for that day. If these totals do not agree, he must check his Daily Allocation Sheets for mathematical errors or recheck the beverage check distribution sheets for missing checks. Proof of the accuracy of his entries is gained only when these totals are in complete agreement.

MONTHLY BEVERAGE CONSUMPTION AND SALES ALLOCATION SHEETS

The information on the Summary Daily Allocation Beverage Sales is transferred daily to the Beverage Consumption and Sales Allocation Sheet for Month as illustrated on pages 154 to 157.

FIGURE 5

Location__ Capital Cocktail lounge __   Station___ 1 ____

SUMMARY
DAILY ALLOCATION BEVERAGE SALES

Date____ June 1, 19 ____   Day__ Wednesday __

ITEM	No. of Drinks Sold	Sales Allocation		Vermouth	Total Sales
Rye	192		$107.80		
Manhattans	148		72.78	26.92	
Rye, bottles	10		87.00		
Totals		Rye	$268.58		$268.58
Gin	99		$ 56.25		
Martinis	115		51.98	19.22	
Other	12		5.73		
Totals		Gin	$113.96		$113.96
Scotch	133		86.55		
Scotch Manhattans	42		26.00	6.50	
Scotch, bottles	8		94.00		
Totals		Scotch	$206.55		$206.55
Bourbon	33		22.10		
Bour. Manhattans	17		9.05	3.05	
Bour., bottles					
Totals		Bourbon	$ 31.15		$ 31.15
Vermouth	9			3.00	
Total Vermouth Sales				$58.69	$ 58.69
				Cordials	
Cordials	50			$32.35	
Cordials mixed (gin)	12			3.42	
Cordials mixed (brandy)	18			6.02	
Totals	80			$41.79	$ 41.79
Brandy	46		$ 27.35		
Other	18		7.78		
Total	64	Brandy	$ 35.13		$ 35.13
Rum	114	Rum	$ 72.55		$ 72.55
Wine	30	Wine	$ 13.45		
Wine, bottles	4	W. Bot.	$ 16.00		
Total wine			$ 29.45		$ 29.45

ITEM	No. of Drinks Sold	Sales Allocation		Total Sales
Draught beer	206	D. beer $ 34.40		
Bottled beer	98	B. beer $ 42.50		$72.90
Total beer		$ 72.90		
Coke, etc.	42	Coke $ 8.40		$ 8.40
Misc.	2	Misc. .70		.70
GRAND TOTAL		$839.37	$100.48	$939.85

Location Capital Cocktail Lounge   Station 1

SUMMARY
DAILY ALLOCATION BEVERAGE SALES

Date June 2, 19   Day Thursday

ITEM	No. of Drinks Sold	Sales Allocation		Vermouth	Total Sales
Rye	170		$ 94.90		
Manhattans	154		75.53	$28.07	
Rye, bottles					
Totals		Rye	170.43		$170.43
Gin	103		$ 58.55		
Martinis	120		54.23	20.07	
Other	7		3.33		
Totals		Gin	$116.11		116.11
Scotch	125		$ 81.25		
Scotch Manhattans	30		17.20	4.55	
Scotch, bottles					
Totals		Scotch	$ 98.45		98.45
Bourbon	40		$ 24.50		
Bour. Manhattans	8		4.35	1.45	
Bour., bottles	2		23.00		
Totals		Bourbon	$ 51.85		51.85
Vermouth	4			1.20	
Total Vermouth sales				$55.34	55.34

(Cont.)

FIGURE 5 (Cont.)

ITEM	No. of Drinks Sold	Sales Allocation			Total Sales
				Cordials	
Cordials	45			$28.00	
Cordials mixed (gin)	7			1.97	
Cordials mixed (brandy)				5.00	
Totals				$34.97	34.97
Brandy	34		$ 17.70		
Other	15		6.50		
Totals		Brandy	$ 24.20		24.20
Rum	92	Rum	$ 56.90		56.90
Wine	25		9.75		9.75
Wine, bottles		W. Bot.		Tot. w.	
Draught beer	220	Dr. beer	$ 37.00		37.00
Bottled beer	103	B. beer	45.55	Tot. b.	45.55
Coke, etc.	30	Coke	$ 6.00		6.00
Misc.	4	Misc.	2.80		2.80
GRAND TOTAL			$619.04	$ 90.31	$709.35

This worksheet enables the beverage cost controller to record each day's beverage business on one line and gives him a
visual picture of the number of drinks sold, their sales value
for any particular day, and the total at the end of the month.

At the end of the month, when the columns are added and
checked, the total of liquor sales for each type of liquor involved in the analysis and the grand total of all liquor sold are
transferred to the Monthly Summary, Liquor Costs and Sales
Analysis (Figure 7).

The final figures in the No. of Drinks Sold columns are
transferred to the Monthly Consumption Control, Liquor
Statement (Figure 8). This statement presents to the manager a detailed record of the consumption, sales, shortages, and
overages for each type of liquor in the entire bar operation.

This statement and the Monthly Summary, Liquor Costs

and Sales Analysis Sheet are made out in duplicate—one copy is kept by beverage cost controller, and the originals are sent to the manager.

THE IMPORTANCE OF PERIODIC AUDITS AND
ACCURACY OF MONTHLY STATEMENTS

The purpose of the Monthly Summary, Liquor Costs and Sales Analysis and the Monthly Consumption Control, Liquor Statements is to provide management with an effective control of liquor costs and to assist in obtaining the highest possible profit on liquor sales. The effectiveness of a cost control system, as outlined in the preceding pages and presented in detail in the following pages, can be measured in proportion to the accuracy of the subsidiary and controlling reports as well as by a thorough understanding of the meaning of the figures in those reports.

The verification of statements and subsidiary records should be the responsibility of the assistant manager. Experience proves that if sales and consumption figures are not properly accounted, manipulations may occur in the Daily Beverage Allocation Sheets and in the figures supporting the allocated sales total and the register reading sales total in the Summary, Daily Allocation Beverage Sales. Other errors may, of course, be found in the Monthly Summary Sheets. These errors, mistakes in addition or subtraction, etc., may occur in the transfer of totals from the Daily Summary to the Monthly Summaries. These errors can be quickly discovered by checking all footings and cross-adding.

Once a week the assistant manager should audit the Daily Beverage Allocation Sheets for any one day. He may select a day at random, obtain the checks under audit for that day, and go through each check, recording on his Allocation Sheets the number and price of each liquor item.

He then summarizes the data on the Summary Daily Allocation Beverage Sales Sheet, compares his allocated sales totals with the sales totals readings of the register tape for that day, and finally, he checks his records with those of the beverage cost controller.

The postings of the totals from the Summary Daily Allocation Beverage Sales Sheet to the Beverage Consumption and Sales Allocation Sheet for the month can be checked in a very short time. The quickest method is to take the Summary

FIGURE 6—BEVERAGE CONSUMPTION AND SALES ALLOCATION SHEET
Month of June, 19__

Location   Capital Cocktail Lounge   Station ___1___

Date	RYE							GIN			
	Drinks		Man.		Bottles			Drinks		Mart. & Other	
	No.	Sales	No.	Sales	No.5's	Qts.	Sales	No.	Sales	No.	Sales
June 1	192	107.80	148	72.78	10		87.00	99	56.25	127	57.71
2	170	94.90	154	73.53				103	58.55	127	57.56
3											
4											
June 30											
Total	4344	2532.40	3020	1483.10	22	12	312.40	2222	1152.80	2480	1152.70
Transfer Row	A	1	B	2	C	D	3	E	4	F	5

FIGURE 6—BEVERAGE CONSUMPTION AND SALES ALLOCATION SHEET (Cont.)
Month of June, 19__

Location Capital Cocktail Lounge   Station 1

SCOTCH						BOURBON							VERMOUTH	
Drinks		Scotch & Man.		Bottle 5th		Drinks		B. & Man.		Bottles No.			Drinks	
No.	Sales	No.	Sales	No.	Sales	No.	Sales	No.	Sales	5th	Qts	Sales	No.	Sales
133	86.55	42	26.00	8	94.00	33	22.10	17	9.05				331	58.69
125	81.25	30	17.20			40	24.50	8	4.35		2	23.00	316	55.34

3096	2013.60	720	432.00	16	179.00	924	547.20	250	134.00		8	96.00	6470	1140.30
	G		H		I		J		K			L		M
	6		7		8		9		10			11		12

FIGURE 6—BEVERAGE CONSUMPTION AND SALES ALLOCATION SHEET (Cont.)
Month of June 19___

Location   Capital Cocktail Lounge   Station   1

Date	CORDIALS						BRANDY			
	Drinks		Mixed (Gin)		Mixed Brandy		Drinks		Mixed Other	
	No.	Sales	No.	Sales	No.	Sales	No.	Sales	No.	Sales
June 1	50	32.35	12	3.42	18	6.02	46	27.35	18	7.78
2	45	28.00	7	1.97	15	5.00	34	17.70	15	6.50
June 30										
Total	1045	662.75	190	53.90	330	110.20	880	495.50	330	142.00
Transfer Row	N	13	C	14	P	15	Q	16	R	17

FIGURE 6—BEVERAGE CONSUMPTION AND SALES ALLOCATION SHEET (Cont.)
Month of June, 19___

Location   Capital Cocktail Lounge   Station   1

RUM		WINE					BEER				COKE, Etc.		MISC.		Total
Drinks		Drinks		Bottles			Glass		Bottles		Drinks		Drinks		Sales
No.	Sales	No.	Sales	Size	No	Sales	No.	Sales	No.	Sales	No.	Sales	No	Sales	
114	72.55	30	13.45	26oz	4	16.00	206	34.40	98	42.50	42	8.40	2	.70	941.85
92	56.90	25	9.75				220	37.00	103	45.55	30	6.00	4	2.80	709.35

				26	32	128.00									
2268	1423.90	605	255.20	Spl.	40	32.00	5112	857.00	2412	1056.60	865	172.80	80	35.00	16,600.35
S	18	T	19	U	V	20	W	21	X	22	Y	23	Z	24	25

FIGURE 7—MONTHLY SUMMARY, LIQUOR COSTS AND SALES ANALYSIS
June 30, 19___

Location   Capital Cocktail Lounge   Station 1

Cost Analysis	Rye	Gin	Scotch	Bourbon	Vermouth	Cordials
1. Beginning Inventory	425.04	221.40	245.00	132.75	114.24	116.37
2. Purchases	1,220.00	861.10	1,020.00	307.98	416.16	258.60
3. Total available	1,645.04	1,082.50	1,265.00	440.73	530.40	374.97
4. Ending Inventory	359.74	349.35	425.13	198.33	214.54	104.11
5. Cost of Liquor Sold	1,285.30	733.15	839.87	242.40	315.86	270.86
6. Sales Analysis						
7. Liquor, Sales, June	4,327.90	2,305.50	2,624.60	772.00	1,140.30	830.85
8. Ratio cost to sales	29.7	31.8	32.	31.4	27.7	32.6
9. Ratio item sales to Total Sales	26.	13.9	16.4	4.7	6.8	4.9

FIGURE 7—MONTHLY SUMMARY, LIQUOR COSTS AND SALES ANALYSIS (Cont.)
June 30, 19___

Location __Capital Cocktail Lounge__   Station _1___

Brandy	Rum	Wine	Beer Draught	Beer Bottle	Coke	Misc.	Total
74.16	210.00	66.92	40.00	142.56	17.52		1,805.96
197.76	408.70	125.74	198.50	367.20	31.68		5,413.42
271.92	618.70	192.56	238.50	509.76	49.20		7,219.38
75.57	157.36	70.18	69.68	73.39	9.63		2,107.01
196.35	461.34	122.48	168.82	436.37	39.57		5,112.37
637.50	1,423.90	415.20	857.00	1,056.60	172.80	35.00	16,600.35
30.8	32.4	29.5	19.7	41.3	22.9		30.8
3.8	8.6	2.5	5.2	6.3	1.		100.

FIGURE 8—MONTHLY CONSUMPTION CONTROL, LIQUOR
June 30, 19__

Location Capital Cocktail Lounge   **Station** 1

Consumption Analysis	Rye		Gin		Scotch	Bourbon		Vermouth
Size	5th	Qt.	5th	Qt.	5th	5th	Qt.	Qt.
1. Beginning Inventory	18	66	19	30	49	17	12	112
2. Purchases	96	192	24	156	204	48	12	408
3. Total available	114	258	43	186	253	65	24	520
4. E. Q. M. Inventory	35.7	70	12.5	61	85.2	25	10.4	210.2
5. Total consumed	78.3	188	30.5	125	167.8	40	136	311.8
6. No. of drinks, Qts.	6,016		4,000			435		9,978
7. No. of drinks, 5th	2,004		781		4,297	1,024		
8. Total drink consumption	8,020		4,781		4,297	1,459		9,978
9. No. straight drinks sold	4,344		2,222		3,096	924		
10. No. mix. drinks sold	3,020		2,480		720	250		
11. Total straight and mix.	7,364		4,702		3,816	1,174		9,705
12. Conv. fac. (.98) appl.	7,514		4,797		3,893	1,199		9,903
13. No. drinks sold by bottle	563				410	256		
14. Total drinks sold	8,077		4,797		4,303	1,455		9,903
15. Shortage by drink						4		75
16. Overage by drink	57		16		6			
17. Shortage by bottle								2.3
18. Overage by bottle	1.8		1/2					

FIGURE 8—MONTHLY CONSUMPTION CONTROL, LIQUOR (Cont.)
June 30, 19__

Location Capital Cocktail Lounge   Station 1

Cordials	Brandy	Rum		Wine			Beer		Coke
5th	5th	5th	Qt.	Sp.	5th	Qt.	½ bbl.	Bottle	Bottle
27	18	11	29	16	29	14	4	792	438
60	48	24	48	48	24	24	10	2,040	792
87	66	35	77	64	53	38	14	2,832	1,230
24.3	18.5	12	21	24	21	18.5	3.4	406	240
62.7	47.5	23	56	40	32	19.5	10.6	2,428	990
		1,792			624				
1,605	1,216	588							
1,605	1,216	2,380		624			5,088	2,428	990
1,045	880	2,268		624			5,112		
520	330								
1,565	1,210								
1,597	1,234	2,314		637					
				40 sp. 32/5ths					
1,597	1,234	2,314		637			5,112	2,412	865
8		66							
	18				13		24		
			2.					16	125

Daily Beverage Allocation Sheets for three consecutive days in the month and check each posting against the Beverage Consumption and Sales Allocation Sheet for that month.

The Beverage Consumption and Sales Allocation Sheets may be checked in a few minutes by totaling the number and sales of any two types of liquor and comparing the figures with the totals posted.

Although the responsibility for the periodic audit rests with the assistant manager, the primary responsibility for the accuracy of the statements of consumption and sales and the subsidiary records rests with the beverage cost controller. To ensure accuracy, the beverage cost controller must perform the following duties in connection with each record.

ACCURACY OF DAILY SHEETS

1. The Daily Beverage Allocation Sheet
   a. Make sure that all checks for the previous day's liquor sales are available.
   b. Read through each check and systematically record the number and price of each liquor item sold in the appropriate space provided for that type of liquor.
   c. Multiply the price of each item by the number sold and subtotal the number and sales of liquor in that particular group.
   d. After all groups have been subtotaled, but before sales are allocated to the liquor ingredients, total all sales and compare with sales recorded by the readings of the register tape. (The total sales calculated and the register tape record of sales must agree.)
   e. Allocate group sales to the various liquor ingredients in proportion to the cost of individual ingredients, or according to the determination of management.

ACCURACY OF THE SUMMARY OF DAILY SHEETS

2. The Summary Daily Beverage Allocation Sheet
   a. Transfer subtotals, number and sales, of all groups to their respective columns on the Summary Sheet.
   b. The Summary Sheet has 4 columns: the number sold column, 2 columns of sales allocation, and 1 column summarizing the total sales of each group. Check each entry for accuracy and for proper transfer to each column.

c. Total each column of sales allocation and the total sales column. The totals of the two sales allocated sales column. This total should be equal to total sales recorded by the register tape.

For example, in the summary of Daily Beverage Sales (Figure 5), the total of the first column of allocated sales is $839.37 and the total of the next column is $100.48. The sum of these totals equals the grand total of $939.85 in the last column.

ACCURACY OF THE MONTHLY CONSUMPTION AND SALES ALLOCATION SHEET

3. The Beverage Consumption and Sales Allocation Sheet
   a. Transfer all subtotals, number and sales, of each liquor group to their appropriate columns on the Monthly Beverage Consumption and Sales Allocation Sheet.
   b. *Do not* enter on Monthly Sheet the grand total of sales recorded on the Summary Daily Allocation Beverage Sales. Cross-add all sales entered in the Monthly Sheet for that day. Compare this total of sales with the total recorded on the Daily Summary. The two totals should agree.

      For example, the total of all sales entered on the monthly Beverage Consumption and Sales Allocation Sheet for June 1 is $939.85 (Figure 6). This total is equal to the sales recorded on the Daily Summary (Figure 5).
   c. Check all postings in the number of drinks column by comparing the number entered for each liquor group with the number recorded on the Daily Summary Sheet.
   d. At the end of the month, total all columns and record the totals in their respective columns on the horizontal total row.
   e. Cross-add the total sales for each group and compare with the grand total. All sales should be recorded in the total sales column.

      For example, the cross-addition of all the group sales in the total row of the Beverage Consumption and Sales Allocation Sheet for the month of June (Figure 6) should equal $16,600.35, the total obtained by adding the total sales for the month column.

ACCURACY OF MONTHLY SUMMARY, LIQUOR COSTS AND SALES ANALYSIS SHEET

4. Monthly Summary, Liquor Costs and Sales Analysis
   a. After the Beverage Consumption and Sales Allocation Sheet for the month has been checked and proved, transfer all sales by groups to their appropriate column on the Monthly Summary Sheet (Figure 7). To make sure that all dollar entries are properly posted, a transfer row is provided on the Beverage Consumption Sheets (Figure 6). As each sales entry is posted to the Monthly Summary, a check mark is placed under the sales figure that has been transferred. For purposes of reference, letters and numbers have been substituted for the check marks.

   On the Beverage Consumption and Sales Allocation Sheet of June 1 (Figure 6), the total sales of rye, $2,532.40, $1,483.10, and $312.40 (items numbered 1, 2, and 3 in the transfer column) have been added and the total, $4,327.90, transferred to the Monthly Summary (Figure 7) in the liquor sales for June row, and at the same time in the rye column for that month (Figure 7, item 1).

   b. After all sales entries have been posted to their respective columns and in the liquor sales row, the sales entries are cross-added. The total of all sales cross-added (Figure 7, liquor sales for June), $16,600.35, should equal the grand total of liquor sales in the total sales column in the Beverage Consumption Sheet (Figure 6).

   c. The ratio of item sales to total sales measures the effect that each classification of liquor has made on the total sales. The ratio states, for example, that 26 percent of the total sales for June was accounted for by the sale of rye whiskey. The ratio is obtained by dividing the total sales, $16,600.35, into the ingredient sales—in this particular example, $4,327.90.

   d. The figures for the beginning bar inventories in each group are obtained from the liquor inventory books. One inventory book is kept in the accounting office and the other is for the beverage cost controller. The liquor items in both inventory books should be classified to facilitate the postings to the Monthly Summary, Liquor Costs and Sales Analysis.

e. The issue figures are obtained from a summary of the beverage requisitions or perpetual inventory cards. The cards are similarly classified according to the types of liquor under consideration.

f. The total available figures are obtained by totaling the beginning inventory and issues of each group of liquors. The ending inventory figures are obtained from the liquor inventory books or from an ending physical inventory of the bar. The cost of goods sold is obviously the difference between the total available and the ending inventory figures.

ACCURACY OF THE MONTHLY CONSUMPTION CONTROL, LIQUOR SHEET

5. Monthly Consumption Control, Liquor

a. The number of bottles and the number of straight and mixed drinks are transferred from the totals in the Monthly Beverage Consumption and Sales Allocation Sheet to the appropriate column and row in the Monthly Consumption Control Statement.

For example, on the Beverage Consumption Sheet (Figure 6) the 4,344 straight drinks of rye and the 3,020 drinks of Manhattan (lettered A and B, respectively, in the transfer column) are posted to the number of straight drinks sold and the number of mixed drinks sold rows in the rye column of the Monthly Consumption Control Statement. The number of fifths and quarts sold, lettered C and D, are converted into 1 oz. drinks available, and the total is posted in the number of drinks sold by bottle row in the rye column of the Monthly Consumption Control (Figure 8).

b. After these figures have been posted in their respective columns, the transfer row must be inspected for omissions. Under each total column, a check mark (in the illustration shown, a letter for number of drinks and a figure for sales of drinks) must be found. Before posting an entry on the Monthly Consumption Control Sheet, all entries must be checked off. If an entry is not checked, look for an omission.

If no omissions are found, all entries on the Monthly Consumption Report should be checked to make sure that the figures are accurate, and that they are posted in the proper row and column.

c. Row 12 of the Monthly Consumption Control Report must be calculated according to previous determination by management. In all the examples illustrated, it has been assumed that management desires to allow 2 percent (2 oz. of liquor for every one hundred drinks sold) of credit for liquor evaporating, spillage, and coating the bottles. Since a full price is obtained for liquor sold by the bottle, this item is not included in that calculation.

To illustrate, in the rye column of the Monthly Consumption Control Sheet (Figure 7) the

No. of straight drinks sold (Row 9)   = 4,344
No. of mixed drinks sold (Row 10)   = 3,020
The total (Row 11)   = 7,364

Since 2 percent is allowed for spillage or similar loss, the total number of drinks, 7,364, must represent 98 percent of the drinks sold. Therefore, .98 divided into 7,364 equals 7,514, the actual number of drinks accounted for in sales.

The total drinks of rye sold and accounted for (Row 14) is the sum of Rows 12 and 13, or 8,077 drinks.

d. On this same statement, referring to Rows 1 through 8 of the Consumption Report, the figures for Row 1, beginning inventory, are obtained from the inventory books and the data for Row 2 is obtained from the record of purchases in the perpetual inventory cards. Row 3 is the sum of Rows 1 and 2. The end of the month inventory, Row 4, is obtained from the inventory books; the information in Row 5, total consumed, is obtained by determining the difference between the total available and the end of the month figures. The figures for Rows 6 and 7 are obtained by multiplying the number of quarts and fifths consumed by 32 and 25.6, respectively. The total drink consumption is obviously the sum of Rows 6 and 7.

UNDERSTANDING AND INTERPRETING
THE MONTHLY STATEMENTS

Much has been said regarding the importance of accurate figures in the preceding pages, but figures themselves—however accurate—cannot run a business or make a profit. The competent owner, manager, or beverage cost controller must be able to understand what the figures are saying. Because of their experience and records of past reports, top level restaurant personnel should be able to analyze the Monthly Consumption Control, Liquor Statement and the Monthly Summary, Liquor Costs and Sales Analysis Sheet. These figures should reflect business conditions and be used to increase service and profits and decrease costs and losses.

In the Monthly Summary, Liquor Costs and Sales Analysis Sheet, the total liquor cost for the entire operation is 30.8 percent. To the unsophisticated observer, this would seem to be an "ideal" percentage figure. "Why," he will ask, "should I lower my costs further when all of my business associates have a 35 percent liquor cost? If I lower my costs much more, I will only be cheating the customers, and sooner or later my sales will decrease."

In answer to that statement, it is entirely within reason to lower costs below the stated liquor cost figure and still increase sales and service. No bar operation is perfect, first, because the people in the organization are human and will make mistakes and, second, because conditions, i.e., costs, tastes, economic conditions, clientele, consumption, and inventories are constantly changing. As personnel make mistakes or conditions change, the costs increase and the gap between sales and net income closes. Third, and most important, the 30.8 percentage is an average.

It is not enough for management to determine arbitrarily a certain range of liquor costs (for example, 30.5% to 31.5% liquor sales) and do nothing as long as the total liquor costs remain within that range. A blanket percentage determination may, and usually does, cloak a multitude of unfavorable conditions that affect sales, service, and costs.

A cursory examination of the two statements reveals several conditions that exist in the operation which have either lowered sales volume or increased liquor costs. For example, in the Monthly Summary, Liquor Costs and Sales Analysis (Figure 7, Row 7, in the columns entitled Beer), the glass and bottled beer sales for the month of June were $857.00 and $1,056.00, respectively. However, the cost of producing $857.00 of draught beer sales was only $168.82, or 19.7 percent of sales, but the cost of producing $1,056.00 of bottled beer sales was $436.37, or 41.3 percent of sales. Stated in other words, over 81 percent of the draught beer sales represents gross income, whereas only 58.3 percent of the bottled beer sales represents gross income, a profit difference of approximately 23 cents on every dollar sale.

Checking Rows 15 to 18 on the Monthly Consumption Control Sheet, Figure 8, reveals that the 16 bottles of beer short are not enough to account for the high bottled beer cost of 41.3 percent and that the 24 glasses of beer over were not the cause of the low draught beer costs.

The fault evidently lies in the relationship between the price and cost structure. Too many of the patrons appear to be dissatisfied with either the amount or the price of the draught beer and have shifted their purchases to the high cost item, bottled beer. (Assume for a moment that the prices at present are 15 cents for 6 oz. and 20 cents for 8 oz. of draught beer.) The beverage cost controller under the direction of the manager should prepare a report showing the effects of changing the draught beer prices from 15 and 20 cents to 10 and 15 cents, respectively. The report should include data on relative and total costs, anticipated sales increase, and shifts from bottled to draught beer sales.

To show more conclusively the unfavorable conditions that are hidden under the 30.8 percent cost figure, the consumption of rye and rum is analyzed below.

The Monthly Consumption Control Report (Figure 8) shows an overage of 57 drinks of rye and a shortage of 66 drinks of rum. Since approximately 3/7 of the total rye drinks consumed straight and mixed consists of Manhattans, the analysis should take into account the factors that enter the mixed drink picture.

On Row 15 in the vermouth column, the figures indicate that there was a shortage of 75 drinks of vermouth. The experienced beverage cost controller can immediately reconstruct the circumstances under which the overage of 57 rye drinks and the shortage of 75 drinks of vermouth occurred. The evidence points to the fact that the bartenders have not been measuring the drinks as they have been directed. That is, 1 oz. of rye and 1-1/2 oz. of sweet vermouth for every Manhattan made. A possible explanation– last month's report showed the high cost of rye; knowing this, bartenders may have attempted to lower rye expenditures by increasing the proportion of vermouth to rye.

The overage of 16 drinks of gin seems to verify this conclusion. At the next bartenders' meeting, the beverage cost controller or the head bartender should state that under no circumstances are the proportions of liquor ingredients to vary from the standard formula.

In the instance of a 66 drink shortage of rum, a similar analysis can be made. If previous Monthly Consumption Control Statements show that the 2 percent allowance for spillage and evaporation is not too low, then the shortage can be explained only by the conclusion that either the rum was sold over the bar and the sales not registered or that the bartenders were not measuring as directed.

All experienced bartenders believe that they can pour a 1-oz. drink by "eye," and some undoubtedly can. However, management should insist that the standard practice of measuring apply to every bartender in the operation.

The two statements, the Monthly Summary, Liquor Costs and Sales Analysis and the Monthly Consumption Control should be analyzed separately and in conjunction with one another. Each statement pinpoints certain conditions that can be remedied, and the statements analyzed together bring out other conditions. Competent analysis will not only reveal these conditions, but also will indicate to management the action needed to rectify the situation.

To illustrate: on the Monthly Summary, Liquor Costs and Sales Analysis, the average inventory of rye is $392.00 and the cost of rye sold is $1,285.30. Therefore, the inventory was turned over three times in one period. Other items, bourbon, for example, show an inventory turnover of less than two. Why is this turnover so low? Can it be improved? What should be done? Who should do it?

Many times, if the first question is answered, the answers to the remaining questions may not be necessary. For example, the beverage cost controller may reason as follows: "Where our minimum and maximum inventory levels are followed, liquor turnover is a function of sales. In this case the sale of bourbon accounts for only 4.7 percent of our total liquor sales or $242.40; yet, because of repeated requests for named bourbon brands, we must keep a certain minimum of name brands in inventory to satisfy customers' requests and maintain service."

The important idea behind the analysis is to find the unsatisfactory conditions that exist in the operation. Once the problem or condition is known, management can decide on the action that must be taken.

A comparison between purchases and cost of liquor sold, rows 2 and 5, Figure 8, may reveal other problems. If the minimum and maximum inventory levels are properly determined, and purchases are made according to these determinations, these two rows should vary little.

The purchases of $197.76 worth of brandy and the cost of brandy sold, $196.35, compare very favorably. In fact, the relationship is ideal. The comparison between the purchases of $1,220.00 worth of rye and the cost of rye sold, $1,285.30, may be consistent with past records. However, what is the reason for the $180 difference in the purchases and the cost of scotch sold? Is this consistent? Should maximum inventory levels be lowered?

The answer can sometimes be found in the changes of inventory. In this case, the ending inventory of scotch has increased approximately $180. Did this increase bring the inventory up to par, or did the increase load the inventory with dead stock? Does this increase represent a special deal regarding price? The beverage cost controller must supply the answers by checking purchase and inventory records.

Similarly, many other unsatisfactory conditions may be brought out into the open. Rows 8 and 9 of Figure 7 show the percentage of total liquor sales each group of liquors accounted for and the portion of costs that was made to bring those sales into being. Rye, for example, accounts for 26 percent of the sales and 29.7 percent of costs. Is this consistent? Are the sales dropping or rising? Trends in sales or cost can be determined by comparison with previous reports. Reasons for sharp differences in cost can be found in the Monthly Consumption Control. For example, if rye costs were regularly 30 percent, the 3/10 of 1 percent drop can be explained by the overages, i.e., 57 drinks. The reason for the overages was detailed in the preceding pages.

In the same manner, each liquor cost item on the ratio cost to sales row or ratio item sales to total sales row should be analyzed. What are the highest liquor cost items? On row 8 the percentages show that the highest cost items are bottled beer, cordials, rum, scotch, and gin, in that order. What can be done to lower costs? In the instance of bottled beer and rum, management decided to shift the sales volume to draught beer, or lower cost item, by lowering prices and seeing that all directions regarding measuring liquor ingredients are followed.

The shortage of 8 drinks of cordials is not sufficient to raise the liquor cost percentage to any appreciable extent. Therefore, the solution to the problem of lower costs must lie in the price and ingredient cost relationship. However, since the price of each drink sold is determined after considering cost, competition, and promotion (and because of the attendant loss of goodwill or probable drop in sales if the prices of cordials are increased), the prices in this instance may be regarded as fixed.

The remaining factor that should be considered is the ingredient cost. The cost of any individual cordial or drink may be lowered by reducing the amount of liquor given in any straight or mixed drink or changing the proportion of high cost ingredients to low cost ingredients, that is, substituting domestic or cheaper cordials for imported cordials, or investing in inventory to take advantage of special deals offered in large quantity purchases. The competent owner or manager will determine the method of reducing costs after he has considered the special requirements of his individual operation.

The analyses described in the preceding pages are only a few of many that can be made from using the two Monthly Statements.

There are a great many conclusions that can be drawn from these statements that are not readily apparent. The experienced operator or trained beverage cost controller can frequently develop many methods of interpretation that will aid him in his specialized operation.

The basic methods of interpretation, however, involve the use of either proportional or comparative analysis. The proportional analysis is the relationship between the amount of an individual item and the amount of a total or subtotal item in the same statement. An example of this analysis is the relationship between the cost of liquor sold and liquor sales shown in the Monthly Summary, Liquor Costs and Sales Analysis Statement, or the ratio of drinks consumed to the total drinks sold on the Monthly Consumption Control, Liquor Sheet.   Comparative analysis describes the relationship between an individual item, or items, on one statement with the same item, or items, in another statement or previous statements in the past, e.g., the relationship between the cost of liquor sold in the Monthly Statement, Liquor Costs and Sales Analysis and the amount of liquor over or short in the Monthly Consumption Control, Liquor Statement, or the comparison between sales or costs of one period with sales or costs of another period.

TAILORING FORMAT TO INFORMATIONAL NEEDS

Although the illustrated forms in the preceding pages were designed to fit the requirements of a specific operation, they could be used effectively and profitably for any bar operation having monthly sales of $15,000 or more.   Ideally, however, the subsidiary records and the monthly reports should be tailored to the requirements of the owner.

The owner may desire more or less detailed information which would depend on individual differences, volume of business, and type of liquor sold. Since the monthly reports are constructed to show at any given time the financial condition of the bar operation, and the subsidiary records are designed to record the data pertaining to how he reached that position, the form of the subsidiary records will depend on the format of the Monthly Consumption Control and the Monthly Summary, Liquor Costs and Sales Analysis.

To illustrate, the owner may feel that the sales analysis summary is important; however, his main problem is theft and/or pilferage of liquor, and he wants to concentrate on that problem now. The owner is stating in effect, that all he needs at the present is the single monthly report—the Monthly Consumption Control, Liquor.

The procedure, therefore, is to eliminate the sales figures from the subsidiary records— the Daily and Summary Beverage Sales Allocation Sheets and the Beverage Consumption and Sales Allocation for the month. The elimination of the sales figures will not affect the usefulness of the detailed information in the Monthly Consumption Control Statement.

On the other hand, the owner may feel that the monthly

reports are not sufficiently detailed. For example, he may want to establish a separate control on sherry, add a liquor group such as vodka, or reclassify wines into domestic—still and sparkling, and imported– still and sparkling. In this instance it is necessary to provide space in the subsidiary records. for the periodic recording of this data. Columns with appropriate headings should be added in the monthly reports to summarize the information.

CONCLUSION

To conclude: the details of cost and the analysis of sales are vital needs of management. A practical, inexpensive, flexible cost control system is an indispensable tool in modern bar operations in terms of increased profits, more effective control, and better administration. Properly used, the information in this section will control the use and consumption of liquor and thereby aid in eliminating theft and waste, determine and promote the effectiveness and relative efficiency of the beverage department, contribute to efficient management at all stages of bar operation, and, equally important, provide management or ownership with data and operational skills to materially increase profits.

The focus of the entire text is on planning for profits. This section on liquor control is no exception. The various informal and formal liquor controls that are described are neither a cost control nor an accounting system. They are specifically organized and incorporated into a single profit control system.

INDEX

ABOUT THE AUTHOR

PETER DUKAS is Director of Florida State University's School of Hotel and Restaurant Management and president of the management consulting firm of Manco Associates in Tallahassee, Florida. Holder of B.S. and M.B.A. degrees from the University of Chicago. Mr. Dukas served as operations analyst for the Brass Rail in New York City in 1951-52 and as manager of Mid City Enterprises in the same city in 1953-54, following which he assumed his present post at Florida State. The author serves on the Board of Directors of the National Council for Hotel and Restaurant Education and is a member of the International Society of Food Service Consultants. He is the author of such books as *Hotel Front Office Management*, *How to Operate a Restaurant*, and *How to Organize and Operate a Restaurant* and has received numerous awards from motel and restaurant associations.